Application Services Library

A Management Guide

Yvette Backer
Remko van der Pols

Van Haren
PUBLISHING

Title: Application Services Library, A Management Guide

Authors: Yvette Backer and Remko van der Pols
Reviewers: Machteld Meijer, Pim Geels, Louis van Hemmen and Mark Smalley
Review coordinator: Bert Franken
Project management: BMG
Publisher: Van Haren Publishing (info@vanharen.net)
Design: BEELDVORM Pijnacker
Edition: First edition, first impression, January 2004
ISBN: 90-77212-03-5

Preface

Information systems have been developed, managed and maintained for decades. Every application management organisation has developed its own methods and so far little effort has been made to standardise the maintenance and control of the application management processes. This is surprising given that application management accounts for a large proportion of IT expenditure. Standard work processes will generally lead to cost reductions. It is therefore sensible, and less expensive, to benefit from the experiences of others.

Fortunately, the tide is turning and there is now an effective option for application management. This has resulted in a process framework and underlying best practices for application management (i.e. maintenance and control, enhancement and renovation of applications). This framework is called ASL (Application Services Library) and is the only public domain application management standard in the world. The framework includes all processes needed to deliver a comprehensive application management service and has been available for several years.

This guide provides an informal introduction to application management and ASL. It was written for business managers who are involved in information technology, IT managers, IT consultants and students. The guide introduces the basic concepts of ASL through realistic situations we all come across at one time or another. The examples are based on VGK, a fictitious IT service provider. The appendices provide a wealth of references to get you started with ASL.

This guide is not intended as reference book, textbook or check list. Its objective is to explain what ASL is and how it can help, rather than how it is done.

Remko van der Pols and Yvette Backer present a book which is easy to read and accessible despite the complex situations that are often encountered in application management. The ASL Foundation fully supports this publication as it provides a good impression of the application management profession and ASL in particular.

I would like to thank everybody who has contributed to this pocket guide, particularly Remko and Yvette, the authors, as well as the review board, Machteld Meijer, Mark Smalley, Pim Geels and Louis van Hemmen, and review coordinator Bert Franken and Herbert Boland, the project manager.

I hope that you will become as inspired by ASL as many before you and that you will be able to benefit from it.

Bilthoven, January 2004
Gert J. van Heun, Managing director ASL Foundation

Contents

What is ASL?

There are many methods that aim to support various aspects of ICT management and ICT service management. The development of structured application management has been rather neglected, compared with the progress made in system development and infrastructure management. The Application Services Library (ASL) aims to fill the gap by providing a framework and a set of best practices for application management.

Origins

Over a number of years the ASL expertise and best practices took shape within one of the largest providers of ICT services in the Netherlands. In 2001 the company decided to hand over to the ASL framework and library over the ASL Foundation, to facilitate the independent development of the standard. The foundation is responsible for the availability, independence, quality, effectiveness and level of the library. ASL is expected to grow and become widely accepted internationally.

Library

The ASL library includes:

- Generic process descriptions of all ASL processes, including the input and output of the processes, activities included in the processes, relationships between the processes, and the roles of the participants.
- Templates for key documents such as annual plans, maintenance plans, Service Level Agreements, files with agreements and procedures, etc.

- Standard reporting agreements with examples of relevant metrics.
- Check lists and other forms of best practices.

The library can be found on the www.aslfoundation.org website.

ASL can help us to realize the following objectives:

- improving cost control;
- understanding the ICT services provided;
- ensuring that expertise is transferred, to safeguard future continuity;
- safeguarding the long-term future of the applications;
- increasing the reliability of the business processes;
- introducing common terminology and concepts;
- supporting continuity and efficiency in a world where business processes are increasingly interconnected in chains.

Getting started with ASL

An organization that wants to get started with ASL can choose from the following options:

- Reading the next chapter to learn more about the ASL approach to application management. The examples will help you understand how your organization can benefit from these concepts.
- Reading about ASL in greater detail. You will find references to other books and articles about ASL at the end of this book.
- Contacting the ASL Foundation and joining it as a participant, knowledge partner or individual member (see Appendix 4).
- Following courses and workshops. EXIN (www.exin-exams.com) has a list of training providers providing courses leading to the ASL Foundation Basic Certificate.
- Contacting organizations who are already implementing and using ASL.
- Undertaking self-assessments and scans.

Introduction to the ASL framework

In the past, the emphasis was always on systems development, rather than on the management, maintenance and enhancement of information systems and applications. Figure 1 illustrates the dangers of this, as most of the costs are incurred during the maintenance and enhancement stages. Fortunately, many organizations are now shifting their emphasis. ASL can support this by providing a thorough and effective method.

	Development →	Maintenance and enhancement
Focus	Major	Minor
Investment	20 %	80 %
Time scale	0.5 – 3 years	8 – 30 years
Users	None yet	Current
Management	Project-based	Line-based

Figure 1 A comparison between development and maintenance

The ASL framework has six process clusters, at three levels (operations, management and strategy), as shown in Figure 2. The six clusters will be discussed in more detail below.

In this guide we will often refer to information systems, we use this term as a synonym of applications, although it is obviously a broader term.

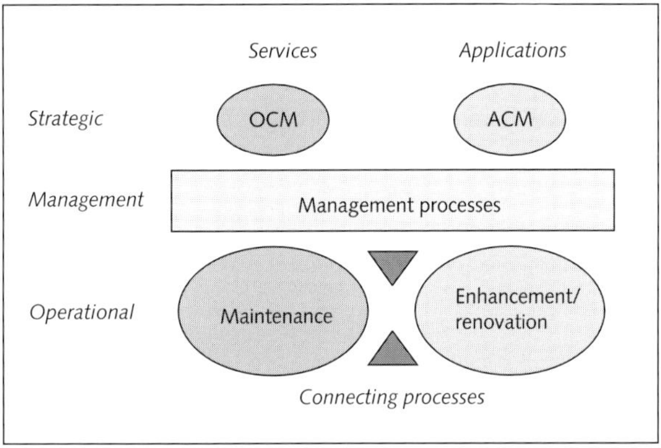

Figure 2 The ASL model

Operational processes

Maintenance

Information systems are created and enhanced in order to use them. This means that they are installed on one or more computer systems and are then started up and run many times, over a period of years, for the benefit of the users in the organization.

The application management organization contributes to keeping the applications up and running. Within ASL, these activities are known as the 'maintenance' activities of application management. Although the importance of these activities is often underestimated they are, in fact, essential: if the information system does not work it is quite likely that the whole user organization will grind to a halt. For this reason, processes such as Continuity Management, Incident Management, Capacity Management, Availability Management and Configuration Management have a significant important impact on the perceived quality.

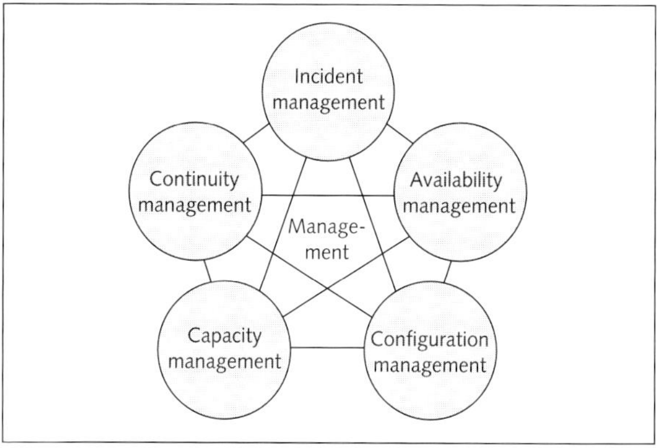

Figure 3 Maintenance processes

Enhancement and renovation

The organizations for which the information systems were originally developed are likely to change. Consequently, their business processes will change and the information systems supporting these processes will have to change accordingly.

This means that the systems need enhancement (others may refer to this activity as 'maintenance'). Both the scope and nature of enhancement can cover a wide range. In some cases the changes to the application will be very minor, such as changes to the screen design or report formats of the information system. However, some changes will be so far-reaching that a large part of the information system will have to be modified. Such a change may amount to a large percentage of the original investment or initial development cost of the information system.

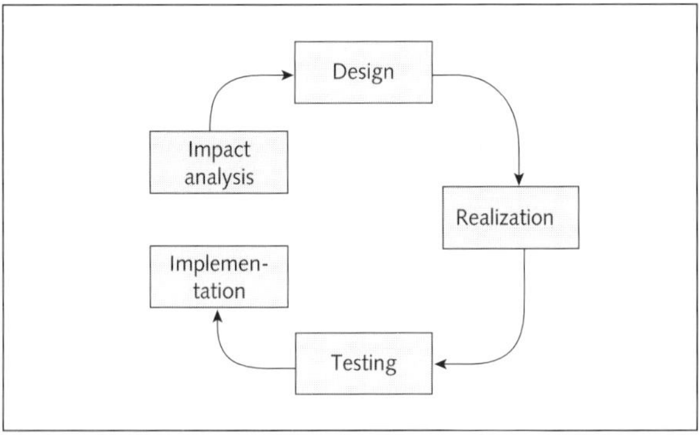

Figure 4 The enhancement and renovation processes

Most of the investments made during the life of an application relate to enhancement and are required for processes such as impact analysis, design, realization, testing and implementation.

Connecting processes

There are links between the Enhancement and Renovation process and the Maintenance processes. In fact, they will often overlap each other, hence there are processes to coordinate them: the connecting processes. In this context the connecting processes are Change Management and Software Control and Distribution.

Management processes

User organizations need the Application Management process to be controlled and managed. They want to know what is happening, they want controlled costs, completion dates and agreements. This is why ASL includes the Management processes.

These are Planning and Control, Cost Management, Service Level Management and Quality Management. These processes control both the Maintenance processes and the Connecting processes and the Enhancement and Renovation processes. This is important as it ensures that the products of Enhancement and Renovation are not simply "chucked over the fence" to Maintenance. This approach also ensures that Maintenance is prepared effectively, even during the Enhancement stage.

Planning and control	Cost management	Quality management	Service level management

Figure 5 The management processes

Strategic processes

Applications Cycle Management (ACM)

One of the issues in maintenance and application management is that it is difficult to take a long-term view (e.g. five years), and there is little innovation. This is unfortunate as over 80 percent of applications will still be routinely used in five years time. ACM, Applications Cycle Management, is the cluster of processes used to develop a vision and policy for the future of the applications and the provision of information. This is done in close consultation with Functional Management (i.e. Business Information Systems Management, which sets the direction of the provision of information to the user organization) and Technical Management (Infrastructure Management).

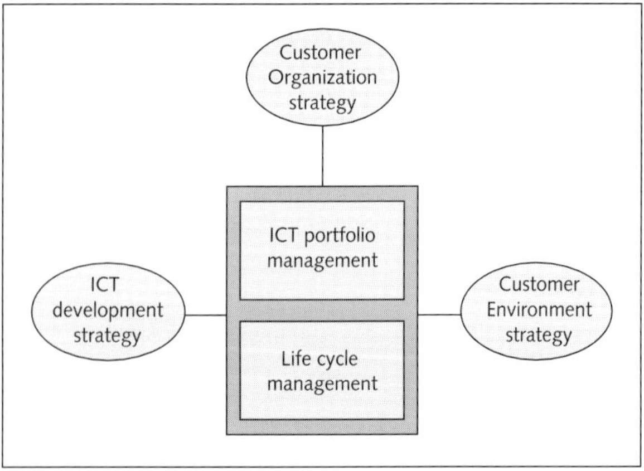

Figure 6 The ACM processes

The objective is to ensure that in another three to five years the applications will still adequately support the business processes of the user organization, and to interpret their requirements in terms of pragmatic and feasible improvements or innovation of the information systems.

Organization Cycle Management (OCM)

It is not only the information systems and applications which change in-line with changing requirements, the Application Management organization itself will also have to change. This is often a major weakness in Application management and Infrastructure organizations.

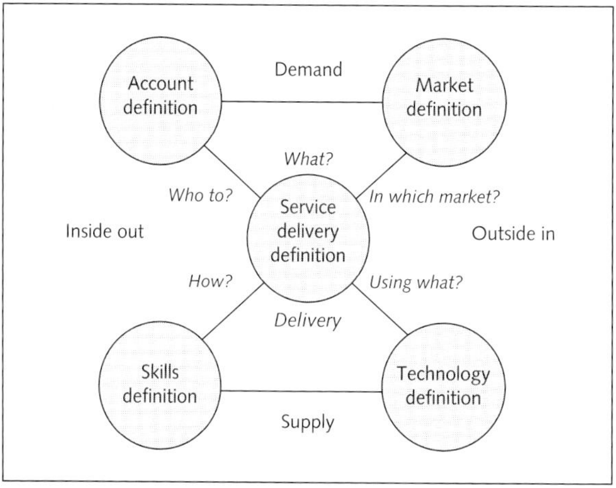

Figure 7 OCM processes

This is the main reason that ASL includes OCM, Organization Cycle Management, which is responsible for innovation in the Application Management organization. This includes the processes Market Definition, Account Definition, Skills Definition, Technology Definition and Service Delivery Definition.

This group of processes defines the policies that the Application Management organization is going implement. The policies are then developed in terms of specific actions, e.g. in the fields of competence development, customer contacts, technology innovation and the approach to the market.

There is a fundamental difference between OCM and ACM: ACM is governed by the user organization and OCM by the Application Management organization. In other words: "What information does the customer want?" and "What services we will be providing?".

The ASL framework

This results in the ASL framework shown below. The processes in each cluster will be discussed in greater detail in the rest of this book.

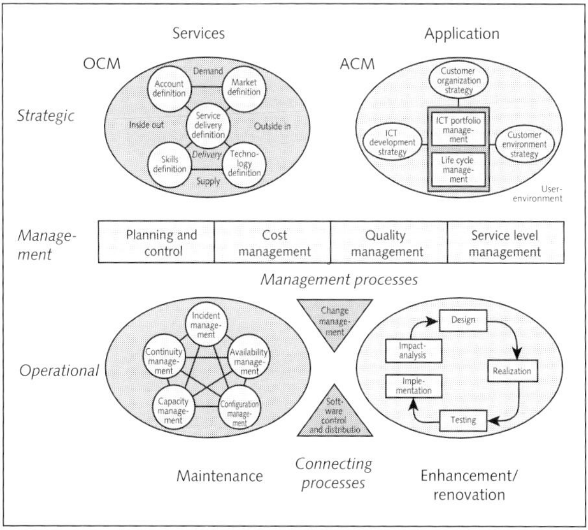

Figure 8 The full ASL framework

Maintenance

Introduction

The day-to-day maintenance (management) of applications is often a neglected aspect of Application Management, as it is normally only associated with the management of the technical infrastructure. However, that is a mistake. Application Management plays a major role in the use and operation of information systems. Some examples:

- Substantive questions about the operation of an information system cannot be answered by Technical Management: the knowledge about the essence of the information for the business processes is found in the application rather than the infrastructure. Consequently, answering such a question demands thorough familiarity with the application.
- Performance is determined not only by the capacity of the infrastructure, but also by the way in which the applications are programmed, and the way in which data is accessed. The system performance will be inadequate if a program uses a poor index or inefficient data access method.
- Experience shows that when dealing with custom systems a large part of the Application Management capacity is devoted to maintenance. This work should not and cannot be undertaken by Technical Management.

The image of the Application Management organization is largely determined by the structure of the maintenance processes and the extent to which the customer's expectations are fulfilled. After all, if an information system is down or defective the fault has to be solved quickly and efficiently. The stability and correctness of an information system do not become apparent during the design stage, but while it is being used. This means that the effective maintenance of an information system is most important.

The objective of the Maintenance processes is to ensure that the applications are used in the best possible way during the operational stage to support the business processes, with a minimum of resources and with the least possible number of operational interruptions. Operating and using applications requires a thorough knowledge of them, and Application Management therefore includes a number of processes to cover this requirement.

The ASL maintenance processes have the same names as the corresponding ITIL processes. The main outlines of the processes are indeed the same, but the way they are carried out is quite different, and there is no umbrella process that covers both Application Management and Technical Management. Consequently, the development of the processes, and the issues they cover, will be different. Using the same names simply makes the interface to Technical Management easier. In many cases (e.g. in the case study used in this book) the applications will often run on several unconnected infrastructures. This is one of the reasons why an umbrella process covering both Technical Management and Application Management would not be feasible.

Maintenance processes

The ASL Maintenance cluster consistes of five processes, all of which are closely connected.

Figure 9 The maintenance processes

The maintenance processes are:

1. *Incident management:* the process dealing with the primary response to queries, requests and faults, including communications with users and Functional Management.
2. *Configuration management:* maintaining up-to-date information about the use and versions of objects related to an application.
3. *Availability management:* the provision, monitoring and assurance of the availability of services and application components.
4. *Capacity management:* ensuring the best possible use of ICT resources, in the right place, at the right time, in the right quantity, and at justifiable cost.

5 *Continuity management:* ensuring the continuity of the operation and support of the provision of information based on information systems.

Incident Management

The essential issue in the Incident Management process is communication with the user organization. Incident Management is a process that also occurs outside Application Management: incident management processes are also used in Technical Management (Infrastructure Management) and Functional Management.

Target group

In Application Management, the primary group addressed by Incident Management is Functional Management, or those in the user organization who undertake functional management tasks. This is different from Technical Management and Functional Management where the communications are primarily addressed to the end users of the infrastructure or the information systems.

These communications can be divided into:

- reactive communications; and
- proactive communications with the user organization.

Reactive communications

Reactive communications are primarily responses to calls and incidents. An incident is a question, requirement, complaint or fault report, generally from a user or end-user. Application Management receives these not only from Functional Management but also from within the Application Management processes (e.g. when it is noticed that the system is running much more slowly than expected), or from Technical Management (e.g. a notification that the application has gone down).

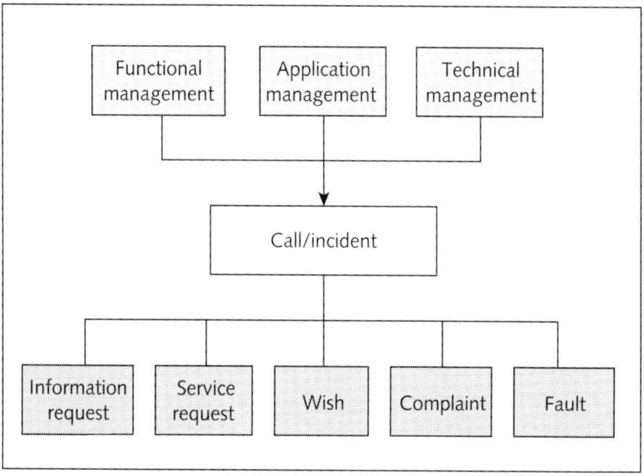

Figure 10 Incidents

The latter aspect underlines that effective coordination of the Incident Management processes between the different forms of ICT maintenance is essential, and that it has to be agreed who will make a call, and when and where.

Proactive communications

The second form of communications is proactive. For example a memo that a new release is about to enter Production, accompanied by detailed information about the new functionality and the way in which it is to be used. This form of communications can prevent much reactive communication.

CASE STUDY: VGK

Tim Clarke only recently became the owner of VGK's Incident Management process. Previously, there was no specific owner. There was a Customer Care Center (CCC) which customers contacted with questions and problems, and the Technical Management Department (TMD) also had a help desk. It was assumed that there was no need for the Application Management Department (AMD) to do anything about this. However, that proved to be incorrect. The CCC forwarded many questions and incidents to AMD. Normally they consulted Henry, Carole or Tim, all three application managers who were thoroughly familiar with the application and the way it was used. However, as no allowance was made for dealing with these questions and incidents, they interrupted the routine work. Consequently, responses were often late or incomplete. Many of the questions from users could not be resolved by the CCC as they required specialist knowledge about the application. John Hollander, AMD's line manager, decided that Henry, Carole and Tim would have to set some time aside for this.

VGK, the fictitious company discussed in this case study, is introduced in Appendix 1.

Furthermore, the functional managers of the customers who run the software on their own systems rarely consulted the CCC but instead contacted AMD's application managers with their questions, incidents and requests for change. Of course, the customers had been informed that the CCC was the initial point of contact. But as customers with questions about the PARIS software were normally put through to AMD they soon decided to bypass CCC completely. Another disadvantage of this was that questions and incidents were not logged by the CCC.

Eventually it was decided to create an Incident Management process within AMD. The department got an incident logging system to record all questions and problems.

The systems were linked so that CCC could see which incidents and questions AMD was dealing with directly. As a result, CCC could keep track of what was happening, and learn from AMD's expertise.

Configuration Management

The Configuration Management process shows what applications are running on what infrastructure by recording these details and providing information when required. This information concerns:

- the information system/application: what is running where?
- the agreed services: which agreements apply where?

The application

For custom applications, running on a central infrastructure, this is a fairly straightforward process, unlike Configuration Management in Technical Management. This is because only one version is used. This process is more complex for organizations that supply packages and for organizations with information systems that run at several locations. For these organizations it is essential to know what versions have been supplied to what locations, what their components are, and what infrastructure they are running on. This information is needed to respond adequately to problems and questions. Analogy: you can only fix a car if you know what make and model it is.

The services

A professional approach requires that it is clear what agreements have been made about particular versions of applications. Detailed agreements about the provision of services and service delivery are also becoming increasingly important. These agreements may be different for each configuration. It is therefore a logical choice to keep information about these agreements in the same place as the configuration details.

CASE STUDY: VGK

At VGK, Harvey Smith owns the Configuration Management process. This process is particularly important as the company's customers use different versions of PARIS, and also run it on different platforms. Most of the customers have contracted the data processing out to VGK, but a few larger customers run the software on their own systems. One of the first things Harvey did was to set up clear records. Some of the problems they had to deal with occurred because they were unaware that a few customers used older releases of PARIS and the database management system. On some occasions they had wasted a lot of time trying to find a bug in the system, only to discover that the customer was using an older version and that the bug had been fixed in a later release. Some time ago they issued a new PARIS release, based on the latest version of the DBMS and using its new functions. This led to serious problems when customers used an older version of the DBMS, as VGK was not aware of that.

Last year Harvey had an argument with William, the Software Control and Distribution process owner. This happened because Harvey also kept copies of all sources supplied to customers. There were a lot of problems with that process. Harvey was missing some sources and quite often he did not receive the patches. He demanded that he should be responsible for all the different versions of the software, so that he would know which version each customer was using. William responded that if Harvey really wanted to do that, he should also be responsible for all test and development versions. Eventually an external ASL consultant was asked to arbitrate. It was decided that Harvey would have to know which release each customer was using, and what platform they were using. They agreed on a uniform definition of the contents of the releases and versions of the software included in each release. As a result, if Harvey needs access to a source, he can just pick up the phone and ask William.

Another problem is that nobody in CCC and AMD knows exactly what service agreements have been made. For example one evening paper publisher has access to the help desk untill 7 PM, while a freesheet publisher is paying for a lower service level and only has access to the help desk untill 5 PM. However, they often call outside office hours as they know the help desk will still be open. These service items really have to be sorted out so that everybody is aware of them, but Harvey simply doesn't have time for that. Discussing this with the Service Level Manager is one of the items included in his improvement plan for next year.

Availability Management

Availability Management focusses on two quality parameters: the availability of the information system and its reliability.

Availability is the extent to which an application can provide the required functionality at a particular time or during a particular period. This relates to starting up the information system, performing the operations at the required time and in the required sequence, dealing with ad-hoc processing requests, availability window of on-line operations, and file retention periods.

Reliability is the extent to which an application or application component provides the agreed or expected functionality, during the specified time window.

Both quality parameters concern both the substance (i.e. the information system or systems) and the service process. Hence, the Availability Management process normally controls four issues.

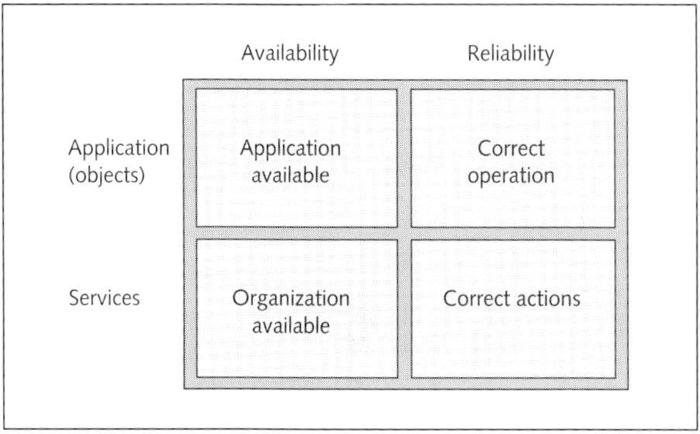

Figure 11 Availability management

Availability of the application

Information systems have to work: within the constraints of the agreements, the users should be able to use the information systems, and processing and other agreed operations should be undertaken at the agreed time. An important topic in Availability Management is ensuring that these agreements are known to those concerned, and that they are complied with.

Reliability of the application

Reliability is important, in addition to availability. It is not enough for an information system to be available, it also has to operate correctly. The number of faults and disruptions during use has a major impact on the quality perceived by the users. A professional approach and continuity therefore demand an understanding of this issue and providing appropriate control.

Availability of the services

It is not just the services that have to be available to the user organization. Agreements also have to be made regarding the services provided by the Application Management organization. The availability of the services refers to the extent to which the Application Management organization is available to the user organization or Functional Management. Clearly, the times at which the help desk is available are relevant, but also whether or not the agreed services defined in the service catalogue (see Service Level Management process) are provided.

Reliability of the services

Although interruptions or the need to ask questions are normally undesirable, they will always occur. It is therefore important that appropriate solutions are provided. The reliability of the services refers to the extent to which the Application Management organization responds to faults, incidents, etc. in accordance with the agreements. Examples of relevant metrics include the MTTR (Mean Time To Repair, the time needed to resolve the bug or disruption), incident response time, etc. The quality and maintainability of the applications is particularly important where these agreements are concerned.

Visibility and practical implementation

Discussions about the quality of the provision of information and Application Management organizations soon lead to issues such as availability and reliability. However, this is in marked contrast with the actual attention devoted to this process and these issues in these organizations. In other words: everybody talks about it, but few do anything about it.

CASE STUDY: VGK

Tim wears two hats: he is not only the owner of Incident Management (a role he was given recently when VGK realized that Incident Management is a process which should be covered by Application Management), but he is also the owner of Availability Management. So he spends a lot of time talking to himself. As the Incident Management owner he thinks that the Availability Management response time is far too long. However, as the Availability Management owner he thinks that it is a waste of resources that they have to start working on an incident within an hour. One of his main challenges as Availability Management owner is that he has to restore PARIS's reputation. At present many customers think that it is an unstable and unreliable application. Together with TMD he has started logging disruptions and problems. The records show that there are indeed many errors in the calculation modules. Many of the other problems are due to the confusing information which TMD receives about how and when the applications have to be run.

Tim is now using information from the CCC and the AMD Incident Management process to get a good idea of the disruptions, stability and reliability of the system when customers run it on their own hardware. Those problems are more difficult to tackle, as it is not easy to determine the conditions under which they occurred. For TMD he has set up a production schedule defining the routine, scheduled and ad-hoc work to be done for the customers whose applications are at VGK. TMD now has a better appreciation of the requirements, as does Tim himself. This has reduced the number of problems.

All these initiatives and reports mean that VGK is now much more aware of quality issues. The reports have also provided input for clearly defined quality improvement projects such as the development of completely new calculation modules, promoted by Reuben Jones. They also want to do more about Availability Management, such as better agreements about the opening times of the help desk, but at the moment they haven't got time for that. The priority is not high enough and there are few Availability Management problems. This means that Tim is going to have a little more time for Incident Management and might feel less like he is developing a split personality.

Capacity Management

Despite the huge increases in infrastructure capacity in recent decades, capacity remains an important topic. This is because the increased capacity is often needed to meet new needs. One tends to associate performance and capacity with Technical Management, but that is only partly correct. The capacity and performance of the information system are also important in Application Management and this issue has to be included in Maintenance for the following reasons:

- The performance of an information system is largely determined by an effective design of the programs and adequate data access by the software.
- Infrastructure was often purchased for the workload estimated at that particular time. This workload may change over time, for example because more and more data is stored in the information system (and it therefore takes longer to find information) or because more complex functions and data queries are used.
- The business process often leads to great changes in the processing volume. Application Management knows how this will impact the infrastructure as this discipline connects the business process to the IT solution.

Consequently, Application Management is also involved in Capacity Management.

Particularly when dealing with larger information systems, Application Management has to be aware of the demand on the information system and how this affects processing. For example, in the payroll system holiday bonuses require a second processing batch which means that the demand on the infrastructure is doubled when the bonuses are paid in June. Hence, the cycle time through the infrastructure might be doubled, or it might be increased by a factor of four or eight. This depends on the design of the information system. Clearly, the infrastructure has to be able to provide the additional capacity.

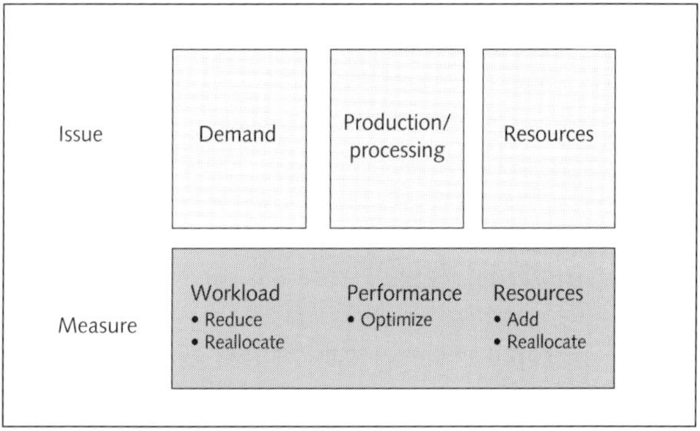

Figure 12 Capacity management

A number of measures can be taken to maintain or optimize the performance, such as deleting unused data, changing the access paths to data, making rows larger, or optimizing the software structure.

CASE STUDY: VGK

Harvey Smith also wears two hats in AMD: he owns both Configuration Management and Capacity Management. This combination of jobs is perfectly feasible. At VGK, Capacity Management is a process that takes little time and causes few problems. Over the past year, Harvey has been receiving monthly reports from TMD about disk space usage and the CPU time requirements of the programs, and these are normally stable and predictable. It wasn't always like that; there have been a number of incidents in the past.

For example, a year and a half ago, they had an argument with TMD. The performance of the programs running in-house had deteriorated significantly as the infrastructure was inadequate. The cost of expansion was so high that the management did not approve it. Harvey was asked to investigate cheaper options that were more likely to continue to be effective in the future. They had known for some time that the performance was rapidly deteriorating as all data, even invoices more than ten years old, was still stored in the system. Consequently they had to develop software to delete old data. However, after the databases had been cleaned the performance did not improve as expected, and was still inadequate. A further investigation showed that a number of access paths were inefficient. They had been set up when the system was first created, and the database contained little data. They had never been updated after that.

To prevent new incidents TMD started providing reports on the software running in-house. This not only increases awareness of the system performance, but also is useful when there are disputes with customers who run the programs on their own hardware. Six months ago there was a major disagreement with some external customers, which was eventually discussed by the directors. The problem was that the new releases had a very poor performance when these customers ran them. According to VGK the problem couldn't be due to the release because Harvey could present the reports proving that there were no problems when VGK ran the programs in house. The two largest customers even threatened to move to a different supplier. The problems were investigated and it appeared that there were actually two causes. Firstly, the customers were using the old version of the database and operating system. However, the optimization depended on features only provided by newer versions of the database environment, which was not used by these customers. Of course, Configuration Management should have been aware of that, and Harvey, as the process owner, dealt with that immediately. Secondly, the job control parameters used by some customers were incorrect. For example, they did not allocate sufficient resources to the software. On top of that, the computers of some of these customers had a fairly low capacity, actually less than required. This meant that they would have to upgrade their systems. Two of these customers then decided to outsource the work completely to VGK.

Continuity Management

Many organizations are critically dependent on their information systems. Developing a new information system requires capital, and the business cannot operate without the applications. Consequently, protection against emergencies and unauthorized use is essential. However, many fall into the trap of assuming that everything will be all right, that nothing will happen. Sometimes they are right, but it is not something you can rely on. This means that the continuity of the provision and processing of information is an essential issue.

Capacity Management addresses the continuity of the information system and information processing. Continuity is the extent to which the information system will continue to operate in the future, without any interruption, or with an acceptable risk of interruption.

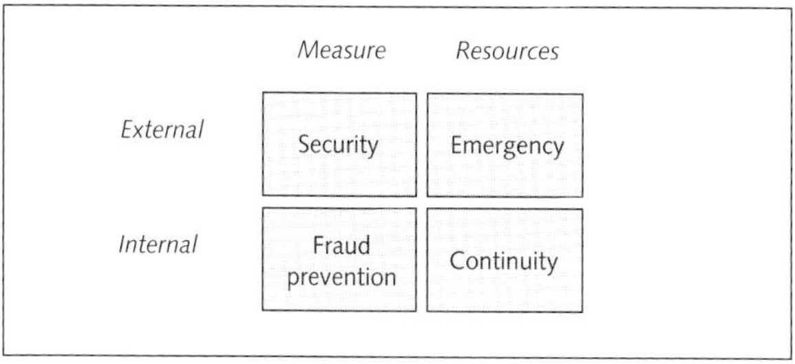

Figure 13 Continuity management

Issues in Continuity Management

Continuity is exposed to a number of threats:

- The information system or systems may be exposed to an external threat, for example someone hacking into an application and using it without authorization. Physical and logical security (effective authorizations, data security, physical security, etc.) can be used as protection against external threats.

- The information system may be used by internal users, for unauthorized purposes. Many information systems deal with large amounts of money and projection against fraud and unauthorized internal use are therefore essential. This often leads to separating functions and authorization structures within the application (information system), clear demarcations between Functional, Technical and Application Management, etc.
- The resources for Application Management and Technical Management may also be exposed to external threats: fires and other emergencies might interrupt the continuity of the information processing. In that event, processing will have to continue at another location. This relates not only to Operations, but also to resources such as documentation that have to be protected against such emergencies.
- The information system is exposed to an internal threat because the resources used are no longer supported. ("DOS is no longer viable", "We've lost the source code")

Technical Management and Application Management

A number of issues, e.g. security and off-site back-up facilities, are provided by Technical Management. However, using resources effectively demands familiarity with the applications, which is why Application Management contributes to this area. For example, Application Management will assist in determining which parts of the information systems need to have off-site back-ups, what essential functionality has to be up and running again within a defined period, etc. The Application Management resources and products also have to be available off-site: source code, documentation and the application development environment are all essential for enhancement activities. Separating functions, authorization structures within systems, etc. are common solutions introduced into the information systems.

CASE STUDY: VGK

Henry has been working at VGK as Application Manager and Database Administrator for over twenty years. He is a quiet and reliable guy who does his work conscientiously. He was always very enthusiastic about the ASL presentations: finally they were going to pay attention to Application Management. Henry was always rather annoyed that most of his colleagues thought that developing new software was much more fun ("sexy") than Application Management ("boring"). He immediately got stuck in when he was asked to take responsibility for Continuity Management. There wasn't actually that much to do, but Henry rather liked the idea of documenting everything so that he could show the rest how carefully everything had been set up.

When PARIS was designed, almost 15 years ago, protecting the system against unauthorized use and fraud was carefully considered. PARIS includes a number of functions with distinct authorization levels. The customers can allocate functions to their personnel, which determine their authorizations. AMD has also taken steps to protect the system. The software is regularly backed up, not just the executables but also the sources and documentation. And of course, they check that the back-up and restore procedures actually work! Henry is always amazed that there are still companies that, after a hard disk crash, discover that the back-up tapes are blank or cannot be restored.

There is also an off-site back-up arrangement for customers for whom VGK runs the software. They have a reciprocal agreement with another software supplier, a specialist in software for logistics and distribution systems, with a similar computer center. All software and documentation back-ups are stored at the back-up location and in the event of an emergency they can install the software and run it. Whenever there is a new release, the new software and documentation are sent to the back-up site. Similarly, VGK provides off-site back-up facilities for the other company. When the agreement was first made they checked if the arrangements worked and how long it would take to resume processing for VGK's customers. Although they worked day and night, it actually took four days to get PARIS up and running again. Henry thinks that there are some opportunities for improvement, and perhaps another practice run would be a good idea.

Enhancement and Renovation

Introduction

The business processes of organizations change over time: they are reorganized, the products or services change, the management model changes, new products or contracts with suppliers or customers are introduced. Consequently, the provision of information also has to change quite frequently. The functionality of an information system is changed in the Enhancement and Renovation cluster.

These processes are very similar to those for developing a new system. That is not surprising given that modifying software requires the same activities, capacity and resources as building new software. Often, a change will amount to building new elements, small or large, for the information system. However, there are also some fundamental differences with system development. These include:

1. Enhancement and Renovation occur within an existing organization, existing infrastructure and existing information system. Hence, there are fewer degrees of freedom.
2. Normally changes are made bottom-up. Ideally a change should amount to only a small modification to one program. If that is not possible the scope widens to a group of programs, or even a whole system component, etc.
3. Maintenance always happens in the line organization. Training personnel to become familiar with the functionality and

structure of an information system costs a lot of time and money. This means that it is difficult to deploy more personnel quickly. Where possible experienced personnel have to remain active in Enhancement and Renovation for a longer period, to reduce the impact of the cost of the training period.

4. Enhancement and Renovation deadlines are often firm. In contrast with systems development, it is not possible to keep the existing information system in operation while the new system is being developed, as it is the existing system that is being modified.

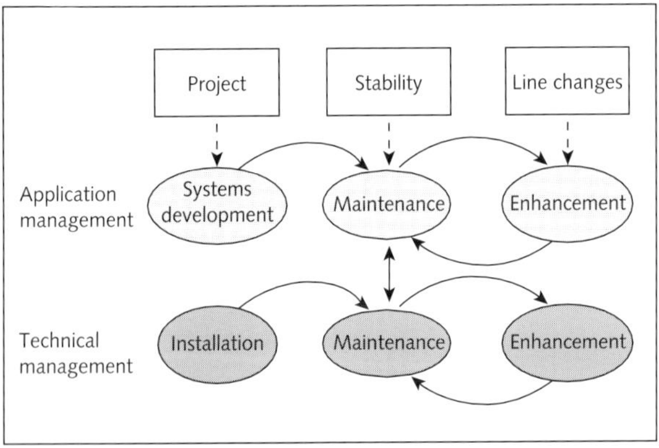

Figure 14 Systems development, maintenance and enhancement

The Enhancement and Renovation cluster includes five processes:

1. *Impact analysis:* the activities to define and assess the impact of the request for change.

2. *Design:* information analysis and design. The activities related to identifying and defining the required functionality.
3. *Realization:* modifying, realizing and assembling the programs (application objects) into applications.
4. *Testing:* testing the modified components and the whole, eventually leading to acceptance and sign-off by the customer of the delivered products.
5. *Implementation:* introduction and roll-out of the modified software and other service components, including dealing with issues such as conversion, acceptance, tests, training, migration, and sign-off.

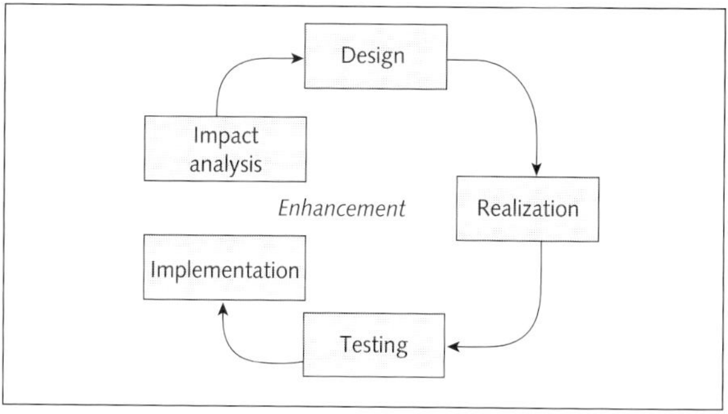

Figure 15 Enhancement and renovation processes

Impact Analysis

The Impact Analysis process is essentially all about "look before you leap". Carefully preparing a release, and considering the requirements and how it will be realized can prevent major problems and excessive costs. Before building the modifications or the release it has to be defined exactly what the modification includes, what parts of the information system are affected by it, what alternatives there are for the realization, what solution will be used, and how the modification or the release will be realized in outline.

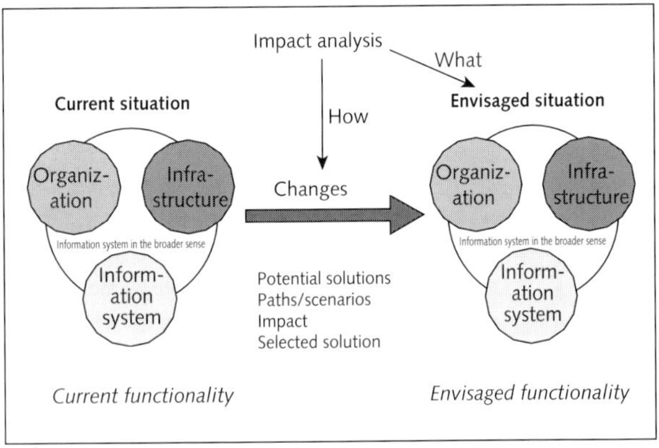

Figure 16 Impact analysis

The objective of Impact Analysis is to answer all these questions. These answers can then be used to make a definite and reliable estimate of the required capacity, cycle-time and planning of the implementation. The Impact Analysis is not limited to the systems engineering aspects. The impact on the user organization, operational environment and long-term enhancement also affect the selected solution. For example, it might be decided to select a solution that is not perfect, and leads to slightly more work by the user organization. In essence, it is all about selecting the optimum solution.

CASE STUDY: VGK

Tony owns the Impact Analysis process and is senior designer of the PARIS team. He has been with VGK for over 15 years and did a lot of work on the original development of PARIS. Two years ago, when John Hollander proposed the introduction of ASL, Tony was not all that keen. He thought that ASL was just going to lead to a lot of paperwork and meetings, which would take up valuable time.

Up until then enhancement rounds were just started with hardly any preparation. Due to the poor definition of the scope at the start and the lack of capacity when it was needed the deadlines were sometimes greatly exceeded, but that was never a problem. The customers were happy, as long as the new functions were provided. And as nobody was concerned about the budgets it didn't matter if they were exceeded.

When ASL was introduced, Tony was responsible for planning a major PARIS release and he thought that it wasn't the right time to introduce ASL. The release was actually fairly disastrous, it looked like they wouldn't meet the deadline and they were well above budget. That led to a lot of problems, as this was the first time VGK had agreed a fixed price and couldn't ask the customers to increase the budget. The deadline was also inflexible as it was based on changes in legislation that was coming into force on January 1. All these problems led to some awkward questions from the management.

There were a number of reasons for the problems, the budget was not detailed enough, the modifications affected a larger part of the system than expected, and the planned solutions were ineffective as they had not been properly discussed with the programmers and technical managers. Finally, in the middle of the design process, one of the designers suffered heart problems and handing the work over to his replacement was difficult due to inadequate documentation. Tony regularly worked till midnight to try and reduce the backlog, and decided he never wanted to go through that again.

During the evaluation meeting for the release it didn't take John Hollander any time to persuade Tony of the attractions of a good impact analysis and preparation for the next release. Tony's next step was to take a few weeks to write a procedure, template and check list for the impact analysis. When it was time for the next release he made a thorough impact analysis. Much to his surprise he discovered that the proposed solution would not be practical. He was relieved to discover that early, in the past they would probably only have noticed it when writing the software. He was even more surprised when the release was finished, as the actual figures were within 5% of the budget, for the first time.

Design

The Impact Analysis process determines the background of the change, the requirements and solution for the modification or release in general terms. The Design process aims to specify the change requirements such that the required information system functionality is unambiguously identified and defined.

A good design serves several purposes:

- It provides an unambiguous definition of what the (part of the) information system will have to do, so that those building it know what they have to build.
- It aids communications with the client (Functional Management) so that they are aware of what the modification or functionality should include.
- The design and any specifications derived from it can be used as decision documents for the acceptance of the release or the system, and for sign-off.

The current trend is towards shorter and increasingly overlapping Design and Realization stages: rapid prototyping, incremental design, etc.

Information system designs are normally based on two or three types of requirements (the last of which is not always included in the documentation or design):

- the data, constraints, and data relationships;
- the transactions, i.e. the operations to process the data;
- the order in which everything should happen (time line), this is particularly relevant to workflow systems.

CASE STUDY: VGK

Miriam Hill, Quality Manager, took responsibility for the Design process two years ago, as this area needed a lot of improvement. There were no design guidelines, nor were any methodologies used. One of the main problems with the PARIS software was the lack of a complete and up-to-date description of the system. When developing a new release, only the changes were described and the descriptions often referred to several functions. Of course, they always planned to update the system documentation after delivery of the release. However, that was usually the period when they were busy fixing bugs in the new software. And by the time they were finished they had to get started on the next release. As a result, they never got round to updating the system documentation.

When Miriam joined VGK two years ago, she noticed that the out of date documentation resulted in many communication problems, both with customers and within the department. It was unclear exactly what the bugs and requirements were and as a result they often developed new functions using the budget that was intended for fixing bugs. It often took a long time to solve problems, and customers regularly complained about that.

Miriam investigated what documentation would be needed to support the operations, and how long it would take to write it. As she suspected that she would not get approval for the 8000 hours it would take to update the documentation she investigated if there was a tool available for that. Unfortunately, all available tools were designed for other development environments, so she still had to make an investment proposal. As expected, she did not get the full budget approved, but the management confirmed that updating the documentation is very important, and allocated a budget of 1500 hours per year, for the next few years. Before starting work on a new release, they now first update the documentation of elements that will be affected by the new release. One of the advantages of this is that there is no need to include the functions that will be removed, as identified by the Impact Analysis. After three releases they have now documented one-fifth of the system.

Realization

Obviously, the functionality of an information system should not only be designed, but also realized. We need people to set up and program the information system.

Programming can include the modification of existing software or the development of new programs.

Setting up relates to adjusting the environment to ensure that the whole provides the required functionality. Often the descriptions of the way in which data is stored in the information system will have to be updated.

The development methods and the quality of the work are important as they determine the quality of the software produced, and how easy or difficult it is to test. The impact on future enhancements, the extent to which the program or information system can be modified in future, is even more important.

Programming is a profession and uses clearly defined construction principles. A professional approach and standardized building and design methods are essential to facilitate transfer to other programmers. Small programs are preferred because programmers can familiarize themselves with them more quickly. However, experience shows that programs will increase in size due to the enhancements. If this is not carefully considered, current enhancements will make it more difficult to make future enhancements. If software is poorly structured it is therefore advisable to restructure it occasionally.

CASE STUDY: VGK

Reuben Jones is the process owner of Realization, a senior developer, and a happy man. After a serious struggle, during the last three releases, he has now received approval for setting up a new structure for the PARIS calculation module. The customers and his management withheld approval for a year, despite his sound business case. He showed that the maintenance of the calculation modules was now costing far more than expected and there were new incidents with every release. For a few years it had been impossible to get this part of the system up and running without interrupting production. As a result, the cost of any modifications was always much higher than estimated.

Reuben had developed a business case that showed that the investment in the development of a new calculation module would be recouped in two years. But it still took him a year of insistence, and support from Miriam, to get approval. There are far less problems with the rest of the system. Of course, there are still some functions that are unwieldy, too complex and poorly documented, and cause lots of problems, but the calculation module is by far the worst and also needs lots of enhancements.

Reuben thinks that the programming of the PARIS system is actually quite good. The programmers are experienced and know how to do their job and usually develop good and structured modifications. However, he still thinks that it would be a good idea to improve the programming standards and organize a refresher course for the developers. They could improve the uniformity, as everybody tends to follow their own style. That is not a major problem, but it would be easier to hand work over to each other if there was more consistency. However, that is something that will have to wait, as they first have to develop a new calculation module. John Hollander is also happy, they now have time to discuss other things during the departmental meeting.

Testing

Application Management is labor-intensive, complex, and demands complete accuracy. Information systems are rarely built correctly the first time, and even after modification the programs are rarely completely bug-free. A single bug means that the information system does not operate correctly, and this can have extremely serious consequences. This means that the delivered products have to be tested. Effective testing is the reason that information system that has reached the Enhancement stage often run smoothly.

The Testing process ensures that the delivered software and data definitions correspond with that which should be delivered given the specifications provided by the client, and the design. The Testing process can be structured and refined. There are test methods, tools and approaches that will make it fairly certain that all program bugs are identified and solved. This means that we can deliver software that is almost or completely bug-free, and many organizations do just that. The many examples where it goes wrong are due to allocating too little time, a low priority, opportunism, or plain carelessness.

Especially during the development of new information systems, but also during Enhancement, there is a tendency to try to make up for delays, incurred in earlier stages or processes, by taking shortcuts during testing. Some think that design overruns are acceptable and that "We'll make up for it during testing." However, that is clearly unacceptable: problems at the start increase the likelihood of even more bugs that will only be revealed by testing.

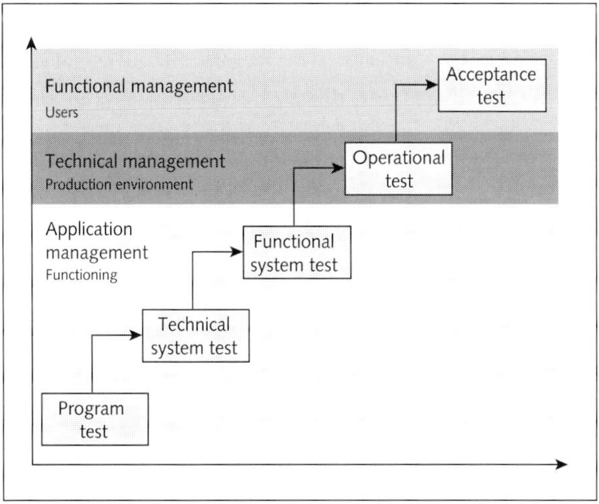

Figure 17 Tests

There are different types of tests, the most important tests are shown in Figure 17. They include program tests (test of new or modified software), technical system tests (technical test of the system as a whole), functional system tests (testing if the system delivers the required functionality), operational tests (undertaken by Technical Management to determine if the software can enter production), and the acceptance test. During the acceptance test the functional manager verifies that the product is delivered in accordance with the agreed specifications.

The last two tests are outside the scope of the ASL framework, which is limited to Application Management. The acceptance test is the responsibility of Functional Management, and the operational test is the responsibility of Technical Management. Of course, Application Management will have to support the relevant organizations during these tests. The program test is included in the Realization process.

CASE STUDY: VGK

Two years ago Paul Green, one of the designers, was asked to become the owner of the Testing process. He was not that keen as he thought testing was by far the least interesting aspect of enhancement, and he knew little about the latest developments in this area. Through Miriam he got into touch with a testing expert at the company she used to work for. After a chat on the phone the expert said that there would be some opportunities to improve the testing process at VGK and they arranged a meeting.

The first thing Chris, the testing expert, asked was how PARIS was actually tested. Paul explained that once the design had been handed over to the developers, the designer would draw up a test design. The test design identified the modified functions, and how they should be tested. Of course, developers would test the modified software themselves, before handing it over to the designer. The designer would then check if all changes had been made correctly, and if there were no problems the software would be handed over to the customers.

Chris then asked Paul what the customers would then do with the software, but he didn't know that. Paul thought that the customers would probably test the changes, just as VGK had done. But he also admitted that the customers would probably use different criteria, such as performance and user-friendliness. He remembered a problem that occurred a few years earlier. They had developed an advertisement-reporting module for one of VGK's other software packages. It was a comprehensive report, with all the information the layout department needed, and it was easy to understand. It had taken two developers over three months to build. The function accessed many tables and was quite complex. VGK were really proud when they presented the module to their customers. Unfortunately they got rather a cold shower, as the customers were far from happy with the reporting module. It took over an hour to generate the report, which conflicted with the layout department's tight deadlines.

Together with Chris, Paul wrote a list of potential acceptance criteria to present to the product consultants and their customers. For the eight customers running PARIS on their own systems they also included additional reliability criteria. When starting work on the next release they agreed test criteria for the new and modified functions with the customers and product consultants. The next step was to decide how to run the stress test that was necessary given the new acceptance criteria. Fortunately that was another area where Chris had a lot of experience. Paul gradually discovered that testing was far more interesting than he had ever thought. Now, two years later, he is one of the most enthusiastic and active advocates of the Testing process.

Implementation

The last step in the development of new releases (or new systems or subsystems) is the implementation. The Implementation process includes all activities needed to effectuate the requests for change from Change Management for operations and data processing. The objective of Implementation is to provide the conditions for the reliable use of the new application and the completion of the Enhancement process.

This process is primarily focussed on realizing the required changes in the Application Management environment. The activities mostly concern support (the actual work is the responsibility of Technical Management and Functional Management, not Application Management). There are also activities focussed on completing the new release.

The introduction of a new release or system often brings with it changes to the production environment of the information system or the way in which Technical Management operates the information system. Conversions (of the data stored in the information system, due to changes to the data model) may be needed, or the control of the processing operations of the information system may change.

Application Management can often support this activity: the required changes are clearly identified, or software is written to bring those changes about. The required changes in Operations will also have to be communicated clearly, and how the interrelationships have changed.

The new release may also affect the user organization. This can result in a lot of work for Functional Management. For example, an acceptance test will have to be carried out to test the operation of the system from the user's view, and further to which the new release will be signed off. End-users also have to be informed about future changes to the information system and how they have to deal with them. Application Management will therefore often have to provide support or information.

Additionally, the change cycle has to be completed within Application Management. For example, the modified application objects have to be archived, the project documentation has to be finalized, and the sign-off has to be documented and communicated. The Maintenance processes also have to be informed of the changes and the expected impact on Maintenance and Operations. All these activities are included in the Implementation process.

CASE STUDY: VGK

Almost immediately after joining VGK, a year ago, Jim offered to become the owner of the Implementation process. As nobody else at VGK, including Miriam, knew exactly what to do with that process they were delighted with his offer. Jim is young, clever, ambitious and keen to learn. At his previous employer's he learned just what could go wrong when delivering software, and it rather looked like VGK were not doing much better.

He dived straight in. He started by setting implementation dates for the customers who relied on VGK's hardware, and the Service Level Manager was not that happy about that. It also made life more difficult for the customers, they couldn't just decide at the last minute that the release had to go into production; instead they had to draw up a schedule.

However, TMD was now able to make proper plans and allow computer time to run the conversions. This meant that they could now guarantee the time required for introducing a new release. Jim also made sure that AMD would write the required conversion software or scripts. Previously, AMD had given the conversion specifications to TMD and the customers who would then write the conversion software. Problems with the conversions often delayed the introduction of a new release. Furthermore, the external customers did not always have the resources to write the conversion software, which led to further delays.

As it was not unusual for VGK to forget to transfer some software to the production system or to the release CD-ROM, Jim introduced a new process stage "Completeness check" and wrote a checklist for it. He also introduced a "Change Newsletter" in which the Change Manager and the developers explained how the new software was controlled, and what resources it required.

There were some who were not that keen about the energy of their new colleague, especially if it meant a lot of work for them. However, John was impressed and gave Jim his full support. In the last few months the relationship with TMD has clearly improved and the operational departments of the external customers are very happy with the delivery of the latest releases.

Jim's latest improvement is the "User Change Newsletter" which explains to Functional Management how the changes in the upcoming release will affect the use of the system. This newsletter is published in HTML format that makes it very easy for Functional Management to distribute it to the help desk and end users over the Internet. Jim is now planning the "Management Newsletter" to inform the management of the user organizations about the new releases. John is not so sure about that, he doesn't know if they will be really interested.

Connecting Processes

Introduction

It was concluded in the preceding chapter that organizations change, and that these changes require changes to the information systems. These changes are made by modifying information system components in the Enhancement and Renovation processes.

Often there will be several enhancement rounds simultaneously, rather than just one. For example there may be a serious disruption due to a program bug. In that case the disruption has to be resolved quickly. This results in two change processes, and essentially two parallel enhancement 'projects', progressing at a different pace.

During these enhancement rounds the same object may be modified twice. This will lead to overlaps: one programmer makes changes for the Enhancement and Renovation round while at the same time another programmer modifies the program to fix the disruption. Consequently, the change made in response to the problem will not be automatically included in the enhancement version.

This means that we need processes to coordinate all these changes with each other and with Maintenance. These processes are known as the Connecting Processes which serve to connect the Maintenance Process and the Enhancement and Renovation process.

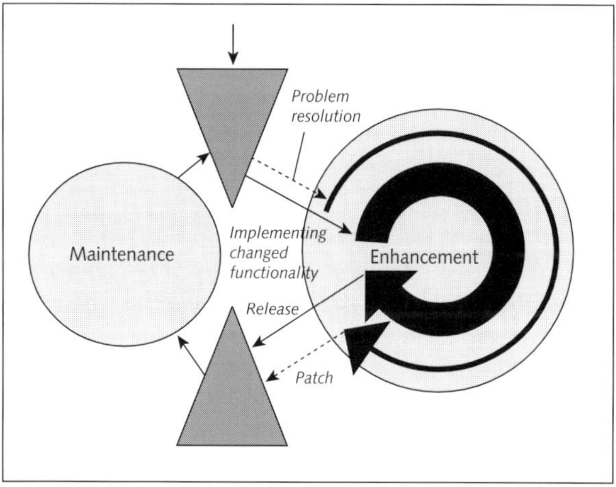

Figure 18 Complexity of the connecting processes

These connections are provided by two processes:
Change Management is the process to identify, prioritize, initiate, evaluate and control the changes to the application.
Software Control and Distribution consists of the activities for the control and distribution of operational application objects (e.g. programs, documentation, data definitions and test sets).

Change Management

The Change Management process is a central element of Application Management. The objective of Change Management is to ensure that a standardized method is used to make changes to an application, so that they can be coordinated and prioritized. In this way, the functionality of the application is improved in the long term.

Change Management schedules the key activity of the Application Management organization: making changes to an information system. The Change Management process collects, administers, prioritizes and schedules the changes to be made.

There are different types of changes: required changes to the operation of the information system, new information system functionality, emergency changes or fixes (changes to deal with problems or faults which affect the operation of the information system).

Normally the Change Management process includes at least three stages to facilitate scheduling:

- changes which have been received, but not yet rejected or scheduled (requests for change);
- changes included in the Enhancement process (in progress);
- completed changes (rejected or implemented).

Application Management professionals often refer to “releases”. Here, a release is a set of changes that will be implemented simultaneously, as a group. Scheduling changes as part of releases has a number of advantages:

- The use of releases results in a more considered selection of what changes will be made when. It improves prioritization.
- The disciplined scheduling and combining of changes means that better use is made of the Application Management resources. For example, if there are two changes to be made to

the same component of the information system, only one test will be required as both changes are tested together.

- The process is more disciplined and it is easier for the user organizations to schedule their work. This benefits quality (everybody knows that an acceptance test will be undertaken on date X, users know that a new release will be rolled out in July, etc.).

CASE STUDY: VGK

Pilar Rodriguez owns the Change Management process and also undertakes the necessary work for it. She took the job over last year from Mohammed Saleh, when he took early retirement. She is not quite sure about the early history of PARIS, but she has heard some interesting things about that period. Apparently, customers and users would simply call the designers to discuss changes, and in the end nobody knew exactly what was included in the upcoming release. And as nobody kept track of what parts of the system were being changed it was not uncommon for several programmers to make different changes to a module. For example, during a change round, a field was added to a screen, then in the next round a new validation was added to that screen, and finally the screen text was changed separately. All these changes were known when they started on the first round and could have been implemented at the same time. That would have meant one test and one hand-over, instead of three. William once joked that it was rather like the public works department in the town where he lives, they would break up the road to work on the sewer, pave it, break it up again to replace the gas pipes and then pave it again.

When he became responsible for Change Management, Mohammed started by collecting all requests for change. After that they could divide them into groups. That was not too difficult, but it was much harder to allocate the changes to enhancement rounds - with 22 customers it is difficult to set priorities. AMD solved the problem by allocating that responsibility to Product Management. After a year they introduced a proper release system and now most of the changes to the new releases are planned at the start of the year so they know what resources are needed, and when. Pilar is now concentrating on the changes to be included in the releases. It is still difficult to get the customers to agree on that. She would like Product Management to take the lead in that and is planning to discuss the issue with them.

Software Control and Distribution

Software Control and Distribution can be seen as the logistics function of Application Management, the warehouse. Software Control and Distribution stores and distributes the various versions of the application objects, such as the information system documentation (e.g. the designs) and the software (the programs). Software Control and Distribution ensures that the right versions of the right application objects are made available to the right persons at the right times. It also ensures that the right versions of the software are supplied to Technical Management.

Several different releases may be prepared simultaneously, as described earlier in this chapter. It is therefore quite possible that there are objects which were modified in a different release, but which have not yet been transferred tot he production environment. The Software Control and Distribution process identifies overlaps between releases. These overlaps need special attention as the different changes made to various objects have to be synchronized in the logistics process.

Example: introducing a patch

A program is modified because a disruption occurred. A quick fix is made and introduced into production. The program will also be modified as part of a release. There is a momentary lapse of attention and the synchronization is overlooked. When the new release is introduced the bug, which had been fixed, returns.

The Software Control and Distribution process can become extremely complex due to issues like this. It is also one of the most important and least visible Application Management processes, just like logistics and stock management are often invisible in manufacturing companies.

CASE STUDY: VGK

Miriam Hill, AMD's Quality Manager, had always been aware of the need for a good structure for Software Control and Distribution. They were making lots of changes and last year they were even working on two releases at once. Often a program being enhanced would crash production and require a fix immediately. Another problem was that the sources were sometimes in the wrong location so a programmer would make a change to an outdated version of the software. Miriam started a project that took two of their people a whole year. She investigated if there was an off-the-shelf tool that could be used in VGK's software environment.

The first step was to define the different types of changes, such as releases, unscheduled urgent bug fixes, and intermediate releases for less pressing problems. The next step was to define the workflows used at AMD. For example, there is the "Urgent fix" workflow for modifying and supplying a program independent of the releases. Another workflow is "Urgent fix 3" which is similar, but covers all supported versions of the system. Similar workflows were defined for regular enhancements and custom developments.

The activities and checks to be carried out are now structured with the tool's workflow. If a patch has to be made they now use the appropriate workflow. As a result, they now no longer lose any source code. The introduction of all this took AMD some getting used to, and they had to become more disciplined. However, the discipline is actually the least of their problems, as they can no longer bypass the process.

Management processes

Introduction

In the past ten years there has been a gradual change in Application Management methods. Customers clearly need services that are effectively controlled and managed. Customers now demand clarity and fixed price contracts. Customers want to know what they are getting for the money they spend on Application Management.

This has led to the need for clear processes for Application Management and the way it is managed. In ASL, this is provided by the Management processes that address four issues:

- *Time and capacity:* Application Management depends mainly on people. Consequently, managing the human resources, in relation to time spent and hand-over dates, is essential.
- *Cost:* the financial aspects of the provision of information are becoming more and more important. In ASL this is reflected in issues such as cost, cost management and a focus on results and fixed prices.
- *Quality:* the quality of the process and the product (the information system) are essential to success in the short and long term.
- *Service Levels and agreements:* clearly defining the expectations of the customers and users about the services, and considering these in the management efforts, is an important element

in raising Application Management to a higher professional level.

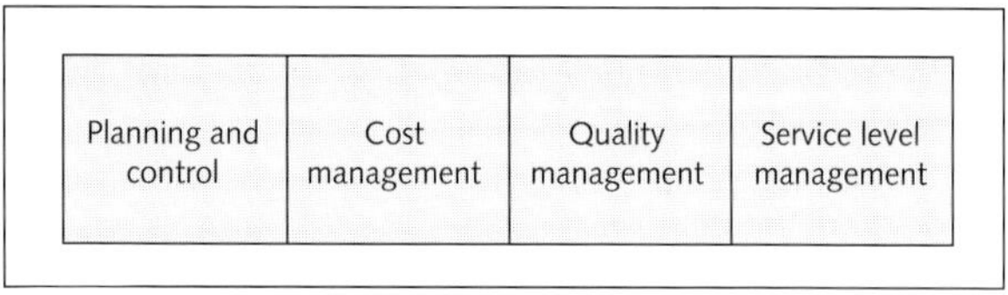

Figure 19 Management processes

Correspondingly, there are four management processes in ASL:

1. *Planning and Control* addresses the use of resources in terms of planning, control and reporting.
2. *Cost Management* is the process that addresses cost control.
3. *Quality Management* is focussed on internal quality, the quality of the organization, products, methods and resources.
4. *Service Level Management* is focussed on managing external quality and the agreements made with the customer.

Planning and Control

There are often fixed deadlines for information systems in the Enhancement stage, for example, new legislation might come into force on January 1, a new insurance policy is launched on May 1, or a new invoicing system starts on July 1. This means that the timely hand-over of new versions of the information system is essential. In the Enhancement stage there is no fall-back, the work simply has to be completed in time. The Planning and Control process aims to ensure that deadlines are met by the effective deployment of human and other resources at the required time.

Planning and Control essentially amounts to management of time and human resources in the broader sense. The deadlines for the delivery of the new services are set in consultation with the client. This means that this process is tightly connected to the Change Management process.

Planning and Control monitors both project work (Enhancement and Renovation processes) and continuous activities (the Maintenance processes). Controlling these simultaneously, often by the same department and the same people, is the major challenge of Application Management. Furthermore, it becomes more complex as there are often additional, non-operational jobs to be done. Examples include improvement projects for Quality Management or Service Level Management and work for the strategic processes included in ACM and OCM.

All these activities demand human resources, Planning and Control is the process to manage them.

This process often occurs at several levels simultaneously: depending on the organization and its size, we have to deal with planning and monitoring a release, planning and monitoring the activities for an application, and planning and monitoring the activities for a release at both the departmental level and that of the Application Management organization as a whole.

The work has to be carried out under many constraints:

- The number of people who are familiar with the information system is limited. It can take a long time for new personnel to become familiar with a system. This means that the enhancement capacity is limited.
- If there is a longer period during which no human resources are dedicated to enhancement of information systems then the expertise will erode. This means that there has to be a minimum capacity (effort) to ensure that future enhancements can be implemented effectively.
- Some skills are not easily interchangeable: good developers are not always good designers or the other way round.

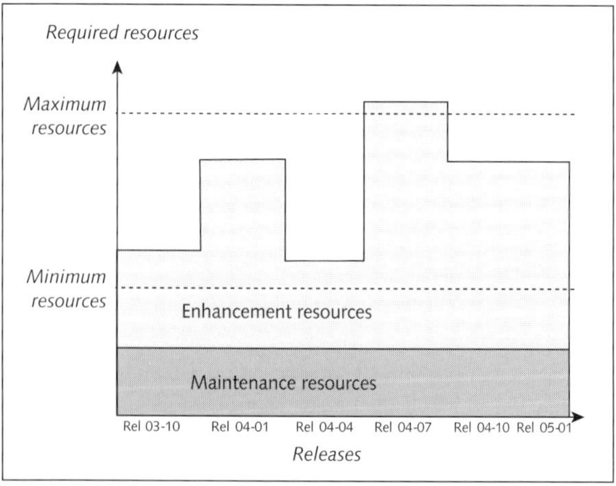

Figure 20 Human resources needs during the life of a release

- The deadlines are often inflexible, as explained above.
- The level of Maintenance activities is fairly stable throughout the year, but peaks may occur due to major disruptions.

This means that effective Change Management is often a prerequisite for Planning and Control as it will reduce the peak workload.

CASE STUDY: VGK

As the line manager with final responsibility, John Hollander is the process owner of Planning and Control. He took on this job two years ago when he initiated an improvement project at VGK. He had always been interested in improving professional practices, and apart from that, the schedules and costs caused major problems.

His first step was to make a separate budget for the maintenance activities. This was because whenever there was a problem, developers had to stop work on the new release and try to fix the problem. That meant the releases were often seriously delayed. Another problem was that other people would not be able to continue working on the release because they were dependent on the input from their colleague who was busy fire fighting.

When planning the last release, John did not commit all of the time of some of his people, so they would be able to deal with problems without delaying their work on the release. The second issue concerned the enhancement budgets. Not only did the projects take longer, they often required several times the planned number of personhours. John had noticed that at the start of a release project they didn't spend enough time and attention on the Impact Analysis. Initially, it took him some effort to get Tony, the process owner of Impact Analysis, to support the improvement efforts. Tony was working on a complex release which, was taking much longer than planned and was way over budget. However, the bright side of that was that it didn't take long to convince Tony that budgeting and planning deserved a high priority. The evaluation of the release showed that the initial assessment of the project was wrong and that they had not recognized the risks. Of course, that clearly showed the importance of an effective and comprehensive impact analysis.

John has now introduced enhancement function scores and standards. The first impression is that they are quite different from what happens in practice, primarily because the complexity of the software is not fully understood. However, John has decided to continue on this track, and undertake a continuous assessment of each release so that they can become more familiar with the new working method.

Cost Management

Often neither the customers nor the functional managers fully appreciate the costs of the provision of information, and the customer has little control over these costs. It is often impossible to link the costs to the services provided.

Cost Management aims to make these costs visible and controllable. In ASL, Cost Management includes the processes for controlling and charging the costs of providing ICT services. This enables Functional Management to take effective business decisions. Policy-related financial issues are outside the scope of ASL. Examples of these include depreciation policies and the cost structure of the hourly rates.

Fixed price contracts

The trend is towards fixed price contracts for services, rather than time and materials contracts as this provides more certainty to customers and Functional Managers. It also provides ICT organizations an opportunity to benefit from any improvements in the processes. However, the disadvantage to the providers is that they are now exposed to risks. It is therefore essential that they set up effective processes. There will also be additional Cost Management tasks. In this situation, the costs of providing the services will have to be managed, and charging methods that suit the customer will have to be developed (e.g. the cost per pay slip or insurance policy, or a fee per user). The actual costs will also have to be compared with the amounts charged to the customers.

	Providing	Servicing	Organizing	Networking
Focus	Focussed on technology	Focussed on providing services	Focussed on processes of the businesses	Focussed on environment of customer organization and the customer's customers
Service	Providing human resources	Providing services	Providing a partnership	Clearing house
Control focus	Quantity	Quality Process design Metrics	Flexibility Effectivity Efficiency	Innovation Added value Social responsibility
Charging regime	Unit rates	Fixed price	Business units	Customer units
Step to take	Process design	Customer focus	Globalization: focus on the customer's customer	?

Figuur 21 Services and growth model

Fixed price models

This development has resulted in a number of different charging and control models for the ICT organization and the user organization.

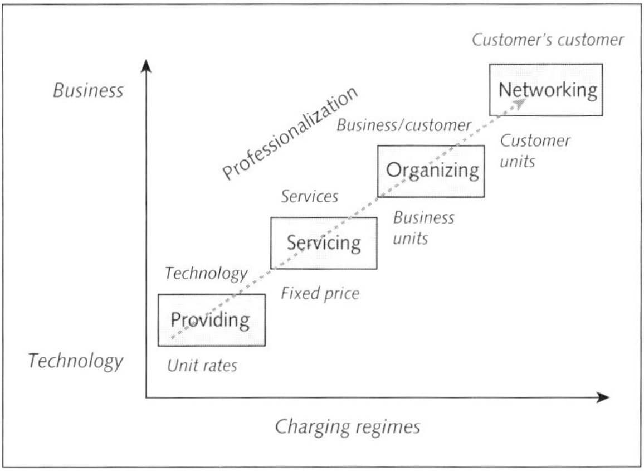

Figure 21 Services and growth model

The way in which Cost Management is implemented also depends greatly on the way in which Application Management is funded (e.g. as a cost center, profit center with neutral budget, profit center) and the cost allocation system. This means that the charging system for the services has to be considered in the context of the way in which Application Management is funded. For example the "servicing" and "organizing" charging models are incompatible with an ICT function funded as a cost center (overhead costs).

CASE STUDY: VGK

Cost Management was introduced relatively late at VGK. Before focussing on the costs they wanted to identify the activities and processes, and control them. Another reason was that VGK was not entirely sure about the cost structures in AMD and PMD. Historically, the situation was quite complex as some customers paid for custom changes. They are now becoming better able to provide cost transparency to the customer. Now that they are more aware of the costs it is becoming easier to give their customers more certainty.

Six months ago, after discussions with the customers, they decided on a better allocation of the risks. The arrangements depend on the type of contract: internal or external. For the internal contracts, PARIS runs in VGK's computer center, and for the external contracts it runs on the customer's own system. There are now clear agreements about Application Management and Technical Management for the internal contracts. It was decided to charge this on the basis of the number of subscribers covered by PARIS. This means that VGK now bears the risk of optimizing the use of computer resources. The external contracts are based on licenses. The license fee includes a fixed element for the use of the software, and a variable charge based on the number of subscribers.

The charging arrangements for the new releases are still under consideration. It is still unclear who bears the final responsibility for the costs of the new release. Within VGK, PMD and AMD disagree about this, and VGK has also to reach an agreement with its customers. On the one hand the customers want VGK to charge fixed prices, but they also want to have a say in what is included in the new releases.

All these agreements have had a significant impact on the way VGK works. They have had to develop spreadsheets to determine if the costs are actually exceeded by the revenues. They also need to improve their awareness of how the costs arise and improve control. It has already become clear that VGK is losing money on the maintenance activities. Fortunately, the improvement efforts are reducing the deficit and in the coming year they even expect a small profit.

Service Level Management

Service Level Management is the process that makes and monitors agreements with customers. The process focusses on the quality perceived by the customer. This contrasts with Quality Management, which is concerned with the *internal* quality of the application and the Application Management organization.

Issues in Service Level Management

Agreements with customers normally cover four areas:

1. The operation of the information system: agreements about the way in which the application should operate. These agree-

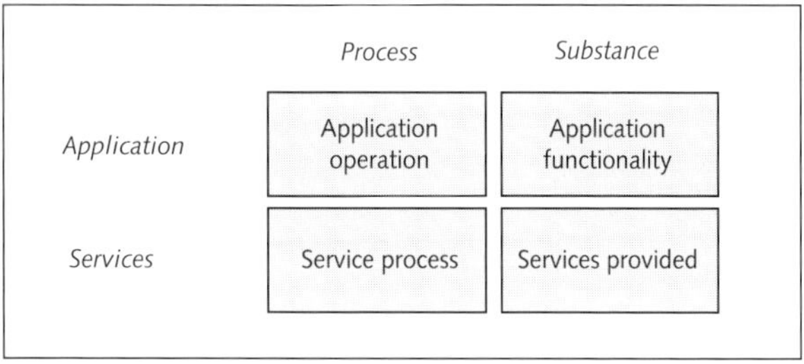

Figure 22 Service levels

ments are related to the results of the ASL Maintenance processes, and cover issues such as availability, performance, reliability, and information system and application security.

2. The functionality of the information system: these agreements cover the functionality of the application and changes to it. Application Management often monitors these closely as they are specified in terms of service levels in approved designs, and checked during acceptance tests etc.
3. The process of actually providing the service: agreements about the way in which the services are provided and about the Application Management organization. These address the access to and availability of the organization, the response time in the event of a disruption, software handovers, process schedules etc.
4. The services provided: the services provided and supplementary services and their conditions - the organization's Service Catalog.

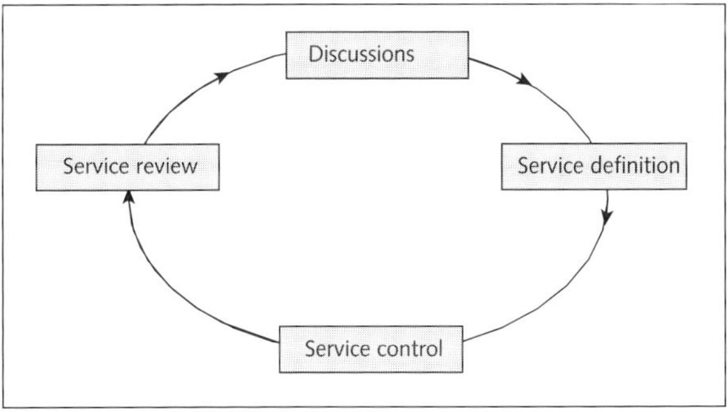

Figure 23 Service level management process

Activities

Like all ASL management processes, Service Level Management includes three activities:

- Defining the service levels: agreeing and defining quality criteria and setting the levels.
- Monitoring the service levels: ensuring that the agreements are fulfilled.
- Evaluating the service levels: investigating the root causes of failure to fulfil agreements and deciding if agreements have to be modified.

The negotiations with Functional Management (the system owner) may precede or run in parallel with the definition of the service levels. Normally, more demanding requirements will result in higher costs. The results of these negotiations, such as contract and SLA (Service Level Agreement) are the primary output of Service Level Management. Obviously, Service Level Management is closely linked to Cost Management.

CASE STUDY: VGK

About eighteen months ago, VGK started concluding Service Level Agreements with the internal and external PARIS customers. The external customers receive the software, install it on their systems and then run it in their own computer center. The internal customers depend on VGK to run the software. The external customers simply get the software and support from the help desk (CCC). The internal customers essentially have an ASP arrangement with VGK who not only develop and maintain the software but also run it on their hardware. VGK concluded the agreements directly with the customers. The SLAs covered issues such as the number of releases issued every year, their contents, the maximum number of problems per year which interrupted production, consistency between the user manual and the software functions, CCC opening hours, etc. For the internal customers there were also agreements about the time at which the work was carried out and how long it would take, response times for interactive operations, and response time to problems that interrupted the production.

AMD then made agreements with PMD about second-line support, budget tolerance for the releases, acceptable number of errors during acceptance, etc. The SLAs covered the operations of the CCC and Product Management but also the quality of the service provided by AMD and TMD. This regularly led to confusion as it was unclear how the responsibilities were divided.

Six months ago they started to set up a clear structure for the Service Level Management process and to review the SLAs. One of the issues discussed was if, within VGK, AMD was a supplier to Product Management. Another question was who TMD's customer was: should AMD provide consistency to the internal customers, or is PMD responsible for that? It was recently decided that AMD is the main contractor and is responsible for the operation, maintenance and enhancement of PARIS. One of the reasons for this decision was that it would ensure that AMD delivers products that run properly and are easy to maintain. This is obviously essential, particularly as there are customers who run the software on their own systems. The cooperation with PMD is now better and the responsibilities are clearly allocated. AMD is now more prepared to take responsibility for the future and the technical quality of PARIS. As most of VGK's Service Levels are provided by AMD, the Production Manager always works together with the AMD Service Manager so they can respond quickly to the customers.

Quality Management

Quality Management often has a thankless task. This is because in the past Quality Management rarely had tangible benefits. Customers and management were often less than cooperative because they thought "it only costs money" and "it just introduces constraints and procedures". However, for a number of reasons, this attitude is now changing.

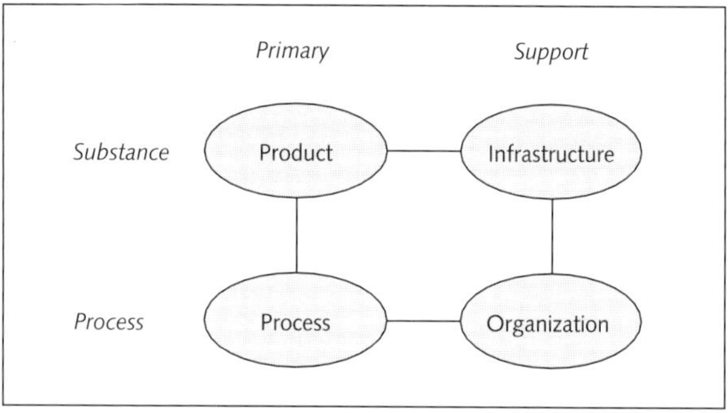

Figure 24 Quality management

Quality Management becomes more practical

It is increasingly appreciated that Quality Management should not be limited to a high level and only be concerned with policies. Quality can become more accepted on the shop floor if the emphasis is placed on practical problems that affect the product and process. Therefore there should be regular reviews within the operational processes to ensure that Quality Management can focus on problems affecting the products and processes, and implement solutions and improvements. This form of problem management is an important element of the Quality Management process.

Internal quality determines the opportunities for the future

The internal quality of the information system largely determines how flexible the information system is, and how easy it is to modify the application. In the longer term this determines the competitive strength of the business process supported by the information system. Customers and users are increasingly aware that overhauls are sometimes necessary. We can distinguish the visible external quality (defined in service levels) and the less visible internal quality. This provides greater support in the organization for quality as a concept.

Issues in Quality Management

The objective of Quality Management is to assure the internal quality of the process and product. It covers four issues:

1. Product quality: the technical and functional quality of the information system and its operation. Normally there are few opportunities for major changes in the short term, as the investments are generally high and the benefits take a long time to materialize. However, in the longer term this quality aspect determines everything else.
2. Process quality: the structure of the delivery process. The enhancement, maintenance and management of Application Management. This is the primary issue when making the organization more professional and improving the services.
3. Infrastructure quality: the quality of the infrastructure used to produce the product and which supports the processes. This relates to a broad definition of the quality system, such as the methods and techniques, and system development tools. In essence the "engine" of Application Management. Policies of ICT suppliers and developments on the market

often necessitate action, such as conversions to upgraded versions and migrations.

4. Organizational quality: this includes the quality of personnel, expertise and the consistency, cohesion and place of Application Management in the organization and its surroundings.

CASE STUDY: VGK

Miriam Hill was hired two years ago, at John's request. Her brief was to introduce ASL to improve the quality of the organization and the processes. One of the first things she did was to identify the owners of the major processes within AMD. The idea was that instead of imposing a method on the organization, she would allow those concerned to structure the processes themselves, based on the ASL best practices. However, it took quite a lot of effort to identify the process owners and to define their tasks, without impinging on their day-to-day work. Miriam usually managed to work quite effectively with John, but they had also had some conflicts as John had a habit of speaking on behalf of the process owners and found it difficult to delegate. On some occasions a process owner had identified and designed a process while John had made different arrangements at the next higher level. That resulted in a lot of tension between Miriam and John. However, after the rather difficult start they now get on very well.

The start of the improvement program was also anything but straightforward: some actions did not lead to the expected result and others were only partly successful. But after a year or so the changes were becoming more successful and there were measurable improvements. So Miriam is actually quite satisfied. Their customers and the PARIS users also confirm the success, although they had little confidence at the start of the improvement program. Right now, Miriam is expecting that there will be major gains from the automated support for the Maintenance and Enhancement processes and continuing improvement of PARIS. However, the investments required for this are so high that she will have to present some convincing arguments.

Applications Cycle Management

One of the major dilemmas in routine Maintenance and Enhancement is that it is limited to a short-time view. Normally, plans are made for modifications to the information system for the next year, but plans covering more than one year are rare. However, the businesses processes will normally change over the course of time. Consequently, the support provided by the information system to the business processes may deteriorate.

Focussing on only one year ahead has many disadvantages:

- Changes are made following an approach that might be incompatible with the development of the business processes in the next three to five years.
- Significant productivity and quality improvements (e.g. restructuring poor software) are never made due to a failure to appreciate that there is a business case spanning several years.
- There is a failure to appreciate that benefits to the business processes can cover a period of several years. Often, changes are not made or it is simply accepted that there is a poor match with the business processes because nobody realizes that the users will be working like this for several years ahead. Often developing completely new software is seen as the only option for long-term improvement, although even in that case, the present system will continue to be used for years.

As a result, the present information system does not meet the requirements of the user organization. This is often solved by building a new information system. However, that requires a major investment (the satisfactory functions of the present system are also rebuilt) and there is always a high risk of failure.

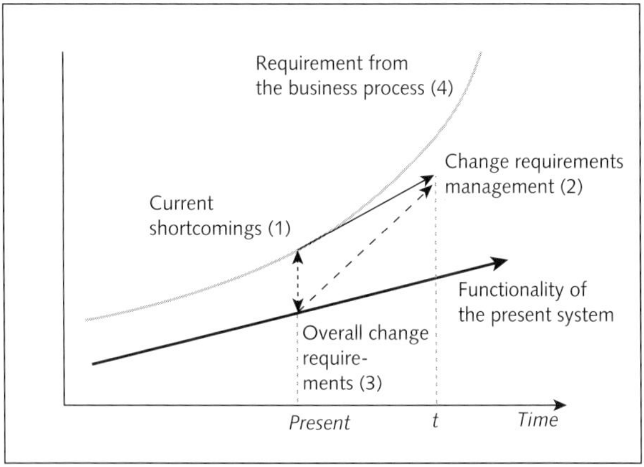

Figure 25 Alignment between the business processes and information systems

To make things worse, in such cases (structural) improvements to the existing system normally come to a halt. And often, the project to build a new system will be less succesfull than hoped for, resulting in a situation that is worse than before.

The Applications Cycle Management (ACM) cluster aims to introduce a strategic perspective into Application Management. ACM focusses on the future of the provision of information and the lifecycle of the objects (applications) that provide that information.

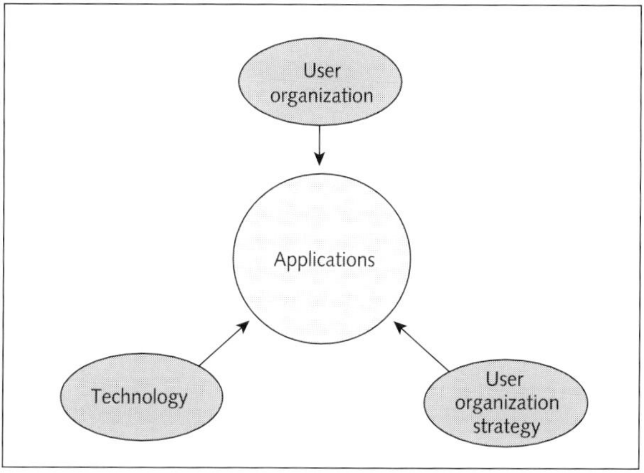

Figure 26 Issues in ACM

There are three external factors that necessitate changes to information systems:

- opportunities presented by technical developments (e.g. system software improvements and the opportunities provided by the Internet);
- changes in the user organization;
- changes in the environment of the user organization.

ACM comprises three processes that aim to understand these developments and determine their impact on the provision of information:

- *ICT Developments Strategy:* the process of monitoring and assessing technical developments.
- *Customer Environment Strategy:* the process of understanding developments in the user organization environment which affect the applications.
- *Customer Organization Strategy:* the process of identifying developments within the user organization(s).

These external factors may affect the applications. However, internal aspects of the applications (quality and cost) can also necessitate major changes. This requires policies at two levels:

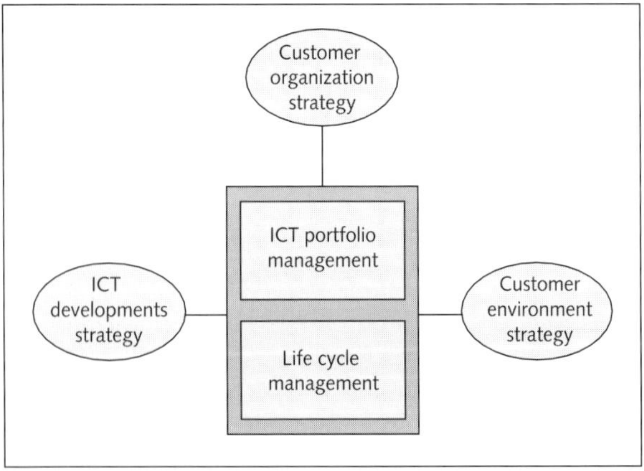

Figure 27 ACM processes

- *ICT Portfolio Management:* the process of defining a strategy for the application portfolio and the provision of information to support the business processes.
- *Lifecycle Management:* the process of defining a strategy for the future of the individual applications, defined as actions.

Although comprehensive new development projects are often tackled top-down, it is useful to opt for a bottom-up approach for ACM, at least initially. This means that the technical, functional and operational quality of the information system in relation to the expected future requirements of the business processes are assessed. The advantage of identifying the strengths and weaknesses of the present situation is that it provides clear information about the feasibility of any changes and the proposed strategy.

CASE STUDY: VGK

Until six months ago, nobody paid any attention to the ACM processes within VGK. John always used to say "as long as we don't know what we are doing, there is no point thinking about what we ought to be doing." However, they have now decided that it is time to introduce ACM, particularly as PARIS is actually quite an old application. There have also been some comments by their customers about the software and their business processes. It is clear that ACM will have to be implemented in close consultation with PMD. Dirk, deputy PMD manager, is the ACM process owner.

As VGK was unsure about how to set up ACM they hired an external ASL consultant. The consultant proposed that instead of setting ACM up as a continuous process, it could be implemented as a recurring project. It would also be a good idea to use external support, as a narrow focus on the current practices might well be a problem. VGK undertook a study with external consultants to identify several options, one of which was then selected in consultation with PMD and their customers.

The main elements of the selected option are:

1. The calculation functions should be improved to reduce the number of errors PARIS produces, to facilitate enhancement, and to improve flexibility.
2. It should be possible to set generic parameters and data to provide greater flexibility to the customers.
3. Additional information will be provided which the customers can use for management information and to facilitate data exchange with other systems.
4. A web interface will be provided for certain functions, so that their customers' customers will be able to access the information.

The investment associated with this option is quite reasonable compared to the other options. These major changes can also be included in the release schedule for the next few years. Their customers are happy with the substantial improvements to the support of their business processes and policies. However, there are still some discussions about the financial aspects. The customers expect that the costs of enhancement will be reduced by the new software structure and off-the-shelf solutions, but it is unclear if that will pay for the new developments. This issue will be settled in the next few months.

Organization Cycle Management

OCM, Organization Cycle Management, is the cluster of processes that aim to define the future provision of services and the structure of the Application Management organization. In essence, innovation should not be limited to the information systems, but also extend to the Application Management organization.

These processes are extremely important to an Application Management organization, for the following reasons:

- user organizations may consider alternative ICT service providers;
- these management organizations are not used to looking at the world outside;
- requirements may change slowly and unnoticed, but they do change.

Relationship between the ICT organization and the user organization

Even when there is an in-house ICT management organization it is by no means certain that it will always be managing the information systems of the business. The relationships between the Application Manager, application and user organization may change. Developments such as outsourcing provide user organizations with an opportunity to become less dependent on internal or external providers of ICT services. Customer satisfaction, image, and good contacts with the user organization are essential to keep the user organization as a customer.

Management organizations are naturally conservative

ICT management organizations are normally very conservative and risk-averse. This is to be expected given the nature of the services they provide: the primary demand of user organizations is that the applications run smoothly. Being risk-averse is therefore perfectly sensible. However, this often makes innovation and change impossible. By contrast, there are also many cases in which new technology is introduced without a careful consideration of the need or costs. This means that ICT organizations have to think about what services they actually want to provide, what services they can provide effectively, and which expertise they do or don't need.

Requirements change gradually

The requirements for the provision of information change only gradually, and there are corresponding changes in the demands made of the service provider. These changes concern the focus on results, costs, efficiency and flexibility, and the services. Normally, the range of services will become broader, but it is often impossible to provide all services that are required. This means that the Application Management organization has to consider which services it wants to provide in-house, and which might require a partnership. The role of the Application Management organization in such a partnership should also be considered.

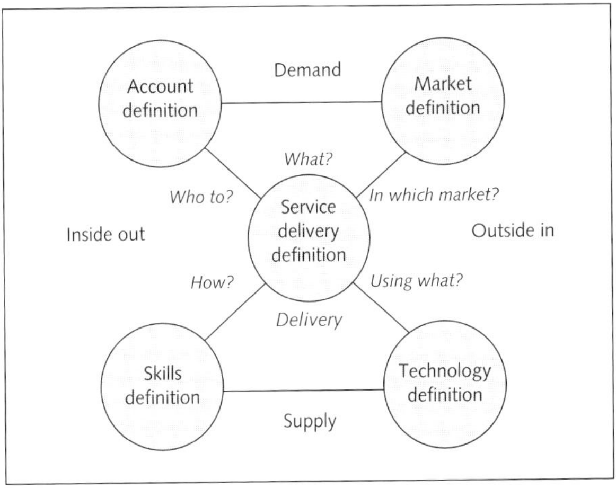

Figure 28 OCM processes

The OCM cluster in the ASL framework includes five processes to ensure that the services provided by Application Management follow the demand from the internal or external market.

Market Definition

The Market Definition process investigates the developments taking place in the market, and their significance for the Application Management organization. This should result in a clear definition of the position of the organization in the field of internal and external providers of ICT services, and any partnerships and alliances.

Account Definition

The provision of services is also affected by the relationships with the user organization(s). This includes issues such as the image of the Application Management organization among the user organization, access to decision makers in the user organization, the account structure, and the services that are or could be provided. Again, it has to be considered whether the portfolio is appropriate, and action will have to be taken to make the necessary changes.

Skills Definition

To ensure that services can continue to be provided effectively in the future the Application Management organization will have to identify the expertise it will need in the future. Making those changes, through training or hiring staff with the required skills, will normally take several years.

Technology definition

Apart from considering the required expertise, the Application Management organization should also set a policy for the tools it uses to provide its services. It is impossible to support everything, and it may take a few years to master development environments, development lines and other tools and methods. Furthermore the cost of acquiring these tools is often very high.

Service Delivery Definition

All the above considerations have to be combined into a clear proposition, a clearly defined range of services, that are appropriate to the market and customers as well as to the in-house skills and tools. This is done in the Service Delivery Definition process.

This process defines the services that are to be provided two or three years into the future, as well as the mission of the organization. After that, the strategy to provide those services is defined. The strategy is then developed in greater detail in the other OCM processes.

Internal and external Application Management organizations

Many of these processes might appear less relevant to internal ICT organizations. For example, Market Definition and Account Definition sound particularly commercial. However, that is incorrect, these processes are actually even more important to in-house Application Management organizations than to external, commercial organizations. External organizations are guided by the demand from the market, whereas internal organizations are less exposed to that pressure. These days, user organizations are less loyal to their internal ICT organizations. They have the option of outsourcing or divesting the ICT department, or just outtask some services. This means that it is essential for internal Application Management organizations to monitor their services, and what they actually offer their customers.

CASE STUDY: VGK

Line manager John Hollander wanted to become the process owner of the OCM cluster, but Miriam was completely against that. She could see his point, but she wanted to make sure that he wasn't the only person involved in this area. As Miriam herself is the Quality Manager and therefore responsible for elements of the process it was decided that Peter would become the process owner. Like ACM, OCM is a cluster of processes that were only recently introduced at VGK. They only felt ready for this during the last year. The company thought a lot about the introduction of the cluster and decided to hire another ASL consultant.

Last month the consultant held an OCM workshop. As recommended by the consultant, everybody participated in the workshop and the day was a resounding success. The management and other personnel were divided into small groups and completed questionnaires. The questionnaires amounted to a basic strength and weakness analysis of a number of OCM elements: customers, market, skills and technology. This produced information such as the contacts in the customer organizations, the image, and the skills available within VGK. There is now also more agreement for example about who AMD's customer is: VGK's customers, or VGK's Product Management which commissions work from AMD. Additionally, the strengths and weaknesses in several areas were identified.

John was pleasantly surprised about the wealth of information his people had about the customers, market and technology. He was even more impressed by the afternoon session in which they discussed the future options, as he realized that his people clearly think in management terms. They appreciate that there are limited resources for investment, and that it is therefore difficult to make choices. The workshop, in which everybody was forced to allocate a limited investment budget, really helped.

Everybody has now agreed about the direction in which they have to proceed, there is a clear vision that everybody supports, and they all agree that the technology and skills should be better aligned with the market. It has also been recognized that the web system that Jim uses for his newsletter could also be used for PR communications with VGK's customers, and may even be relevant to their customers' customers. A small working party is being set up to study the options. It also became clear that some of the programmers need additional training, as the programming language they specialize in will be phased out.

One thing they haven't decided about yet is if Product Management should be invited to the next workshop. However, it is clear that the people in AMD have so much detailed information about their customers and the market that it would be useful to share that with PMD.

APPENDIX 1

Case study: VGK[1]

The discussion of ASL is interspersed with a case study based on VGK, a fictitious provider of computer services to publishers. The company is introduced in this appendix. VGK used to be the in-house IT department of a publishing group formed through the merger of several publishers. Five years ago the IT department became an independent company.

Market

VGK has greatly expanded its market. After the spin-off and further growth, VGK now serves 22 publishers instead of 13, despite the consolidation of the market due to mergers. Their strength was a fairly comprehensive magazine subscription application that suits the requirements of various publishers. This is a fairly specialist market, and the choice of software is limited.

PARIS

PARIS is an integrated subscription software system. It is used by publishers for tracking, fulfillment and billing. There is also a special module for daily newspapers with their own delivery personnel which handles bonus payments and complaints. Because of its clear structure, PARIS can even be used by small publishers who need a comprehensive software package.

1 Please note that VGK is a purely fictitious company and that any resemblance to any organisation or individual is purely accidental.

Strictly speaking, VGK is responsible for PARIS. However, this was not always so clear-cut. Originally, the customers participated in the decisions about its features and costs. However, now that the market has become much broader than the original publishing group, the decisions are primarily made by VGK.

Organizational structure

VGK includes three departments that correspond with the three major management areas.

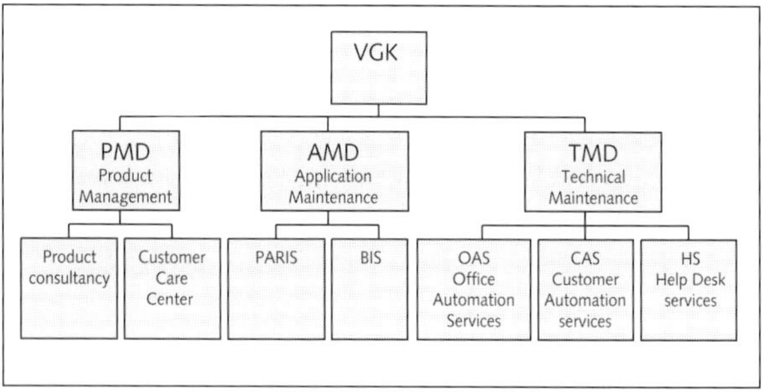

Figure 30 VGK

Product Management Department (PMD)

PMD is the Functional Management organization for PARIS and BIS. Within VGK, this department has the expertise about substantive issues, it is the primary contact for the users, and is the client of the Application Management Department (AMD). The full responsibility for PARIS and its functions is shifting to VGK. Hence PMD will eventually have full commercial responsibility for the costs and revenues of PARIS. However, its internal structure is not yet fully prepared for this. Consequently there is still some overlap with the Functional Management carried out by AMD.

Application Management Department (AMD)

This department is responsible for the maintenance and enhancement of the applications. Within VGK, it is the client for PARIS services. AMD is responsible for Application and Technical Management in VGK.

When dealing with customers AMD is normally supported by PMD. The reason for this is that although PMD is responsible for the provision of PARIS services to VGK's customers, internally AMD is responsible for realizing them. This division has demarcated supply and demand within VGK. This also means that within VGK, PMD is the designated customer representative.

Technical Management Department (TMD)

This department is responsible for the computer center. TMD provides two kinds of technical management:

- Office Automation Services (OAS);
- Customer Automation Services, (CAS): running major applications, such as PARIS, for customers .

CAS plays an essential part in PARIS services, unlike OAS. Hence AMD has extensive contacts with CAS and little contact with OAS.

Services

VGK's customers

VGK has 22 customers who use PARIS. Eight of them run the software on their own infrastructure, in their own computer center using their own hardware and personnel. They occasionally receive new releases of PARIS, which they install themselves. VGK provides Technical Management services for 14 customers. This is provided by TMD under the direction of AMD.

PARIS releases

At present there are three releases of PARIS in use:
PARIS 9.8, PARIS 9.7 and PARIS 8.0. Two customers on their own infrastructure use release 8.0, and it is no longer supported by VGK. These two customers are still using this version as they have not had the time and resources to migrate to the latest release.

There are three PARIS releases every year. VGK schedules the releases in consultation with the customer. The contracts require the customers to follow the PARIS release policy and to be at most one year behind the latest release.

Quality improvement

Two years ago, AMD decided to become more professional. One of the reasons for this development was that they were split off from the ICT organization of the publishing group. The objectives were to control the provision of services more effectively and increase cost-awareness. When other publishers started using

PARIS it became even more important to focus on efficiency and profit. John Hollander was hired to manage this change.

PARIS was originally developed as custom software for just one publishing group. Although it is now used by a number of other publishers, VGK has not fully made the change to becoming a supplier of standard software packages.

APPENDIX 2

ASL and other methods

ITIL and ASL

ITIL, the Information Technology Infrastructure Library, is primarily concerned with Technical Management (i.e. aimed at organizations which maintain the technical infrastructure), whereas ASL is concerned with Application Management (the organizations that maintain the information systems). ITIL is focussed on the computer center and infrastructure, and ASL is focussed on the applications.

To some extent, ASL is based on the ITIL concepts. This is apparent from the names and structure of certain management processes. ASL also uses these concepts, but addresses Application Management, the maintenance and enhancement of information systems. This requires different skills and expertise, and an emphasis on other issues.

CMM and ASL

CMM (Capability Maturity Model) has traditionally been a model for system development organizations (new developments or major enhancement/renovation projects). It identifies five levels of maturity, each of which includes a number of processes. The presence or absence of these processes determines the maturity of the organization.

CMM primarily addresses the management level, rather than the strategic level. It focuses on the Quality Management and Planning and Control processes.

ASL does not use maturity levels for the Application Management organization as a whole. However, there are maturity levels for the ASL processes, and scans are available on the market to identify them. For example, there is a scan to identify maturity levels in outsourcing and for the development of the professional level of Application Management organizations. However, these instruments are not part of ASL.

SDM, DSDM etc. and ASL

SDM and DSDM are both system development methodologies. SDM used to be a popular standard. SDM divides system development into stages, with underlying activities, documents and reports. The stages include definition study, basic design, detailed design, realization, testing, etc. There is also an operations and management stage, but it is rarely used. DSDM can be combined effectively with rapid application development. The stages of SDM and DSDM fit into the ASL framework which means that a modified version of SDM or DSDM can be used for software renovation. Furthermore, many documents (e.g. system documentation) are transferred from the development stage of the system to the Maintenance and Enhancement processes where they are essential.

Yourdon and ASL

Yourdon and related development methods concern the realization. ASL does not specify any particular approach, but does assume that an appropriate method will be used.

Functional Management and ASL

Functional Management (Business Information Systems Management) refers to all the activities undertaken by the system owner. Functional Management personnel look at the organization and specify what the system should do, they support the end users, and ensure that the organization benefits effectively from the provision of information.

ASL does not address Functional Management. However, after introducing ASL there will be a need to make the client organization more professional. This is because after the introduction of ASL, Functional Management may be found to be lagging behind. Some of the potential benefits of ASL will not be obtained if there is an insufficient Functional Management capacity. There are a small number of Functional Management approaches available that can be combined effectively with ASL.

Application Management and ASL

Application Management covers the maintenance, enhancement and renovation of applications. ASL is a methodology for all aspects of Application Management, from strategy to operations.

Technical Management and ASL

See "ITIL and ASL" and "Functional Management and ASL".

Prince 2 and ASL

Prince 2 is a project management method and can be used together with ASL. For example, in Application Management, projects can be set up for major renovation efforts in the ICT organization, and Prince 2 can support these successfully. ASL primarily addresses the operations of the line organization.

ISPL and ASL

ISPL (Information Services Procurement Library) focusses primarily on procurement and defining the delivery of ICT services and therefore has links with application services. It mostly addresses functional management issues and can be used for the more detailed development of ASL processes such as Service Level Management.

APPENDIX 3

ASL Foundation

The ASL Foundation was established in 2002 by a number of vendors and end user organizations who wanted to raise Application Management to a higher professional level. The Foundation has adopted the method ASL (Application Services Library) as the standard for Application Management processes.

Applications generally have long lives, and continuous changes make the operational management and updating of information systems complex and expensive. It follows from this that the control of IT processes has become very important. The Foundation gives professionals who want to improve methods and exchange best practices an opportunity to meet. This cooperation has many benefits as it will be possible to improve work processes on the basis of the experience of others, and vice versa. This will reduce costs and improve the services. Thus the quality of the industry as a whole will be improved.

Activities

The activities of the Foundation include:

- Best Practices
  The participating organizations have committed themselves to contribute best practices. Other organizations can also submit best practices. The Foundation reviews the quality of

the proposed best practices and approved best practices are then published on the web site.

- Training & Certification
  Training personnel in Application Management is essential to ensure consistent terminology. The Foundation ensures that the modules offered by various training organizations are compatible. Training organizations can also apply for accreditation. The exams are organized by Exin, an independent organization. The quality of the Application Management processes in an IT organization can be certified by independent auditors.

- Development
  The Application Services Library is developing continuously and new contributions are always welcome. The Foundation compiles the contributions and helps to improve the ASL framework by organizing themed meetings, discussion groups, etc.

- Publicity
  Effective publicity is one of the key factors in ensuring the adoption of ASL as the standard for Application Management processes. The Foundation publishes articles and books, organizes seminars and presents ASL at network meetings and at interested organizations.
  Most of these activities are free of charge. All publications and standard presentations can be downloaded from the web site www.aslfoundation.org or ordered via info@aslfoundation.org.

Participation

If you are interested in this new standard and want to help improve the quality of Application Management you can participate in one of three ways:

- Individual
  As an individual participant you can join the activities and you will have access to the knowledge network of the Foundation.
- Knowledge partner
  All employees of your organization or business unit will have the same benefits, in your country, as individual participants. Your company name will be mentioned in presentations and on the web site and reciprocal links can be set up.
- Participant
  Participants form the governing body of the Foundation and are committed to providing the human resources to realize the Foundation's targets. They are at the heart of the Foundation on an international scale. Participants are directly associated with the goal of the Foundation: professional Application Management.

For more information:
Website: www.aslfoundation.org
E-mail: info@aslfoundation.org

APPENDIX 4

Sources of information about ASL

Further reading

Pols, R van der, *ASL, a Framework for Application Management*
This book discusses ASL in depth. The processes for the maintenance and enhancement of applications are discussed against a practical background. The introduction of the ASL processes and methods is illustrated using many examples. Published early 2004 by Van Haren Publishing, ISBN 90 77212 05 1.

ASL Self-assesment workbook , ISBN 90 44007 51 3.
This book discusses the maturity and the ASL compliance of your application management processes. It can be very helpful to analyse your application management organization, find bottlenecks and get tips to improve your services.

ASL

Homepage of the ASL Foundation: www.aslfoundation.org.
Follow the link "ASL Publications". The publications in English are listed at the bottom of the page.

OGC

The organization behind ITIL: www.itil.co.uk

Exin

A list of organizations providing training towards the ASL Foundation certificate: www.exin-exams.com.

itSMF

The Information Technology Service Management Forum:
www.itsmf.net (itSMF USA)
www.itsmf.com (itSMF UK and international)

APPENDIX 5

The ASL framework

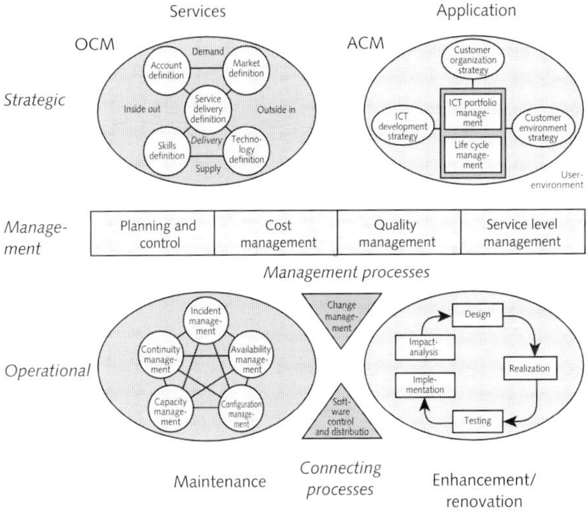